Mihrî Hatun

Gender, Culture, and Politics in the Middle East
miriam cooke, Simona Sharoni, and Suad Joseph, *Series Editors*

SELECT TITLES IN GENDER, CULTURE, AND POLITICS IN THE MIDDLE EAST

Anxiety of Erasure: Trauma, Authorship, and the Diaspora in Arab Women's Writings
Hanadi Al-Samman

Arab Women's Lives Retold: Exploring Identity through Writing
Nawar Al-Hassan Golley, ed.

Beyond the Exotic: Women's Histories in Islamic Societies
Amira El-Azhary Sonbol, ed.

The Female Suffering Body: Illness and Disability in Modern Arabic Literature
Abir Hamdar

Gendering the Middle East: Emerging Perspectives
Deniz Kandiyoti, ed.

Intersections: Gender, Nation, and Community in Arab Women's Novels
Lisa Suhair Majaj, Paula W. Sunderman, and Therese Saliba, eds.

Rituals of Memory in Contemporary Arab Women's Writing
Brinda Mehta

Words, Not Swords: Iranian Women Writers and the Freedom of Movement
Farzaneh Milani

Mihrî Hatun

PERFORMANCE, GENDER-BENDING, AND SUBVERSION IN OTTOMAN INTELLECTUAL HISTORY

DIDEM HAVLIOĞLU

Syracuse University Press

Syracuse, New York 13244-5290

First Edition 2017
17 18 19 20 21 22 6 5 4 3 2 1

∞ The paper used in this publication meets the minimum requirements of the American National Standard for Information Sciences—Permanence of Paper for Printed Library Materials, ANSI Z39.48-1992.

For a listing of books published and distributed by Syracuse University Press, visit www.SyracuseUniversityPress.syr.edu.

ISBN: 978-0-8156-3549-9 (hardcover) 978-0-8156-3537-6 (paperback) 978-0-8156-5415-5 (e-book)

Library of Congress Cataloging-in-Publication Data

Names: Havlioğlu, Didem Z., 1970– author

Title: Mihrî Hatun : performance, gender-bending, and subversion in Ottoman intellectual history / Didem Havlioğlu.

Description: Syracuse, New York : Syracuse University Press, [2017] | Series: Gender, culture, and politics in the Middle East | Includes bibliographical references and index.

Identifiers: LCCN 2017040204 (print) | LCCN 2017042117 (ebook) | ISBN 9780815654155 (e-book) | ISBN 9780815635499 (hardcover : alk. paper) | ISBN 9780815635376 (pbk. : alk. paper)

Subjects: LCSH: Mihri Hatun, 1460?–1506—Criticism and interpretation. | Turkish poetry—15th century—History and criticism. | Women poets, Turkish—Biography. | Gender identity in literature.

Classification: LCC PL248.M48 (ebook) | LCC PL248.M48 Z69 2017 (print) | DDC 894/.3512—dc23

LC record available at https://lccn.loc.gov/2017040204

Manufactured in the United States of America

For my mother, Hatice,
who constantly creates beauty and love
during and after her lifetime

Contents

Illustrations

Tables

Preface

"How dare he!" she grumbled. It had been hours since she left the prince's palace but she still could not get over it. She walked to her window facing the Iris River that cut her beloved city Amasya into two halves. As she glanced at the mosque Prince Ahmed's mother, Bülbül Hatun, built on the riverbank, her heart began to race again. They all had laughed when Makâmî sang his awful rhymes at the meeting. She looked at the piece of paper in her hands on which she had scribbled his lines as soon as she returned home. She read:

> My pledge is this, that I will give my life in exchange for a kiss
> Proffer your lips and don't suppose that Makâmî is a liar.

Each time Mihrî read those sleazy lines, she felt the same rage as when she first heard them. She still could not comprehend how this wannabe poet dared to treat her as a beloved and ask for a kiss! Who did he think he was to use her, the woman poet of her times, to attract attention in the prince's palace? It was the cheapest trick she had ever seen. She usually knew exactly what to do in a situation like this but, for some reason, she was speechless last night. That was likely because she expected nothing like this from a youngster imam.

She began to pace back and forth in her spacious room. The old wooden floor made the usual noises, letting everybody in the house know that she was awake. In a few hours, her handmaid Hatice would knock on the door with warm water for her morning toilette. Thinking about Hatice reminded her of an important errand she needed to take care of today. Hatice's daughter Zeynep was old enough now to attend primary school. She needed to talk to Hoca Efendi at the school because, although she had already taught Zeynep to read and write, a child must socialize with her peers. Growing up in this house among poets and artists, Zeynep did not understand what the real world is like for a little girl.

Just like Mihrî herself. Growing up, she did not know what it meant to be a girl outside of her own privileged life. Her father, Mevlânâ Belâyî, the last male member of a venerable pious family in the city, had raised her after her mother passed away when she was very young. She was his only child. He believed it to be God's will and refused to marry again. He taught her everything he had learned from his father and grandfather and took her everywhere he went, whether it was the Sufi convent or the *meclis* gatherings at Prince Bayezid's palace.

Soon, she had become friends with the prince and the children at the palace. Prince Bayezid was particularly fond of her and another very bright kid, Abdurrahman, from the Müeyyedzâde family. Even though they were younger than him, the prince enjoyed their company while they played in the palace courtyards or learned from the most prestigious scholars of the time. Their favorite was Şeyh Hamdullah's calligraphy hours. They liked making funny faces out of the Arabic letters as the wise Şeyh told them the mysterious stories of the Hurûfî path.

She had been forced to say goodbye to her friends when Bayezid assumed the throne and Abdurrahman joined him in Istanbul later. She remained in Amasya where she belonged. Both her family's and her own name, Mihrî Hatun, were very well known and respected in this city, but she was nobody in Istanbul. When she visited her friends in the sublime city, she was struck by the grand image of Ottoman rule, but she felt very small and insignificant at the same time. In her city, she was a well-known woman poet and the only remaining descendant of the family that founded the Halveti branch.

She began pacing the room once more, counting rhymes and murmuring words. She didn't even hear Hatice's knocks on the door. When she finally dipped her reed into the inkpot, her face brightened with a mischievous smile. That upstart poet Makâmî was going to learn tonight who he was competing with:

The preacher accused us falsely, calling us beautiful
The number one poets are the biggest liars

From now on Makâmî, our only kisses will be
Years of angina and the torment of diarrhea

❀

The brief mention of this anecdote occurring between the woman poet Mihrî Hatun (ca. 1460–1515) and Makâmî (dates unknown), an imam/poet from the same time period, appears in the *tezkires* (biographical dictionaries) of the early modern Ottoman period. My rendering of the story is based on a combination of the scholarship produced in recent decades in the field of women's history and my interpretation of Mihrî's poetry. According to the limited information we can extract from the historical data, we know that Mihrî Hatun hailed from Amasya, a small but influential provincial town in which *şehzâdes* (crown princes) acquired administrative experience by serving as governors. During Mihrî's lifetime, Bayezid II (1447–1512) and his son Ahmed (1465–1513) served as governors. As a result of the royal family's ambitious patronage of the arts and sciences, the city was not only a vibrant urban center for artists and mystics, but also a crossroads for migrants, specifically those coming from the East, namely the Iranian lands. Moreover, the only known women poets before the eighteenth century all came from Amasya.

During his time as governor in Amasya, Bayezid's circle included Mihrî and other notable intellectuals, such as Müeyyedzâde Abdurrahman Çelebi and Tâcîzâde Cafer Çelebi. Bayezid himself received a comprehensive education in both the secular and religious sciences, the arts, and literature. He was a poet and collected his poems in a divan (poetry collection) under the pen name Adlî. Throughout his life, he was a generous patron of the arts and sciences and showed his appreciation by compensating scientists, poets, musicians, and craftspeople with regular salaries. On several occasions, he rewarded Mihrî's poems with monetary gifts, an early example of a woman making money from her poetry. After Bayezid's enthronement in Istanbul, his entourage in Amasya moved with him, including his beloved friend Müeyyedzâde Abdurrahman Çelebi, despite this being against his late father Mehmed II's wishes. Mihrî, on the other hand, stayed in Amasya and continued composing poems under the patronage of his son, Şehzâde Ahmed, the crown prince who succeeded his father as governor in Amasya. Both the Topkapı palace gift registers and the *tezkires* suggest that she was rewarded and acclaimed at the time she was writing.

Although this limited information about Mihrî is extracted from historical documents—most of which appear to have been written as entertaining gossip by male biographers—her divan remains a rare incident in Ottoman intellectual culture. The information we have about women before the nineteenth century is scarce and almost always related by men. Mihrî's divan is a glimpse into a woman's world that has been invisible to outsiders, particularly the male writers of history.

I am far from being the first person to discover Mihrî. She has sparked historians' interest for many centuries. However, what has been written on her has not necessarily been about her; rather, it has been a representation of commonplace ideas and beliefs about women of her time. In that sense, the sexually explicit representation of her by sixteenth-century biographers resembles her positioning as the "Turkish Sappho" by Orientalist historians such as Joseph von Hammer-Purgstall or E. J. W. Gibb, as well as the tendency within modern-day scholarship to interpret her work as imitating the so-called original male poet's voice. The common issue shared among these approaches is that they all reproduce the discourses around gender prevalent at the time they were written, rather than engaging with Mihrî's poetry in its own time and place. In other words, she has been treated as an extraordinary incident simply because the writers of history have known so little about women and were uninterested in Mihrî's own words.

The diminutive and somewhat distorted information I could find about Mihrî—only a few pages in biographical dictionaries—provoked and nurtured my interest throughout the years. Evidently, although there were more than four hundred poets documented during this period, only three of them were women. Soon I realized that this limited information about women poets was not about women in general, but about what it meant to be a woman in the discourse of the court. While thinking about how to engage with her work, it became clear to me that, if I wanted to say something new about Mihrî, I had to bring her own words into the picture. I embarked on a diligent analysis of her poetry based on four manuscript copies, paying attention to the poetic discourse as a tradition and her performance and manipulation of this tradition to carve out a space for herself in the court. Slowly but surely, the text itself revealed to me the gaps in poetic discourse that she masterfully manipulated, allowing her to be a successful woman poet in a male-dominated tradition.

Focusing on Mihrî's writing while considering its intertextuality, this book develops a comparative approach to reading artistic production alongside its close relationship to real life. This approach demonstrates how poetry can have documentary value. What we see today as a written form of rhetorical meditation had a very different function in early modern times. The process of production and performance of poetry in intellectual circles reveals a tradition and lifestyle that can be found in the poetry itself. In the gendered space of court culture, poetry was the battleground on which meaning was negotiated and gender roles were constructed that were, in this period, far from being binary categories. Thus, poetic performance could be subversive within a permissible range of possibilities. A master poet such as Mihrî shows us how it could be done.

As an attempt to contribute to the growing scholarship on women and gender in Middle Eastern and Ottoman history (which has focused on the nineteenth century onward, mainly due to a lack of sources in earlier periods), this book offers Mihrî's poetry as a new source to reconsider women's place in history. Regarding women only in the modern periods and focusing on certain genres, such as novels and periodicals, has forced the scholarship to define women's participation in the intellectual world as part of the project of modernization. Mihrî's story puts itself forward as an excellent case study for reevaluating the question of women before modernity and proposing "a history of their own."

A note about the English translations of a selection of Mihrî's poetry is necessary because of the significant choices made during the rendition from Turkish to English. One point of debate has been how to communicate the lack of gender in the third person in Turkish and the necessary gendering in English. Ottoman poets took advantage of the gender ambiguity in Turkish and, consequently, the gender of the beloved remained cleverly ambiguous. Nevertheless, in English, it is almost impossible to generate similar ambiguity without compromising meaning. For the purposes of this book, I chose to use the male gender, "he," for three reasons: first, the ideal beauty was male and, as I discuss in later chapters, Mihrî did not cross the lines of aesthetic conventions. This does not mean that she did not challenge mainstream poetic discourse. Her subversion appears in the way she clearly identifies her own gender as a woman, rather than hiding the gender of the beloved like a male poet. Second, because the expected norm in poetry was homosocial desire, by being clear about the male gender of the beloved Mihrî generates a rupture and introduces desire between a man and a woman—a desire that was only acceptable through marriage. Finally, although she mentions names of her male patrons and poet colleagues, she never mentions a female name other than calling herself Züleyhâ.

In response to early readers of the manuscript version of this book, the cover image is a detail from a miniature in Ahmed I's album from the seventeenth century. I think it is a rare representation of women in a *meclis* of their own while they collectively read a book. This image represents the unknown world of women and how this book re-envisions that world through Mihrî's poetry.

Acknowledgments

I began this book several years ago, during my first months of graduate school at the University of Washington. I was doing primary readings with Walter Andrews and wondering about the presence of women in Ottoman history. Walter encouraged this interest and, soon thereafter, we started working on Mihrî's poetry every Wednesday morning, a tradition that continued throughout my graduate years. For this, I am grateful for Walter's trust in me from the very beginning and his unfailing support throughout the years. He has been my *hoca* in the Ottoman sense and I believe my poetry analyses clearly reflect his legacy in the field of Ottoman poetry.

This work was made possible by the interdisciplinary training I received thanks to the teamwork of Selim Kuru and Reşat Kasaba. I was one of the students they encouraged to explore and challenge the borders and possible intersections of academic disciplines. I was also lucky to learn from my fellow scholars in various fields during our weekly meetings of the Turkish Circle at the University of Washington in Seattle. Moreover, Leroy Searle's valuable feedback helped me tailor gender theory for my purposes. Stacey Waters introduced me to the ways in which I could make optimum use of the text that this book is based on with the help of the digital humanities. Thanks to his training, I generated an electronic text of Mihrî's divan and used this to make word lists, frequency tables, and clusters, all of which helped me to understand how she used the poetic discourse. I then compared my findings with other texts already prepared by the Ottoman Text Archive Project.[1]

This book evolved from my dissertation project. However, it was only possible to begin contextualizing Mihrî in her time and place with my later work. The first and most important side path that I took was during my postdoctoral fellowship at Harvard University. Cemal Kafadar's work on Ottoman women has been influential and, with the extensive resources at the Widener Library, I could explore the history of women's writing in the Middle East and therefore expand the limits of my dissertation.

Once I began teaching in the United States and Turkey, my colleagues and students had a tremendous impact on my understanding of women in intellectual history. I gained insight from discussions with the students in my classes, which I organized around the major themes of this book. Among many other colleagues, I am particularly grateful to my dear friend Irvin Cemil Schick for our continuous conversations and our collegial collaborations. He has been a wonderful team player in search of creativity and new ideas to explore.

Meanwhile, as a woman in academia, I understand the necessity of mentorship and have been exceptionally thankful for the support of Stacey Katz Bourns and Engin Akarlı. Stacey believes that it is incredibly important to support women scholars, and watching her commitment has been inspiring. Obviously, one does not have to be a woman to support women scholars. Engin Hoca always does his best to include women

1. A sample of the text can be found at the Ottoman Text Archive Project (http://courses.washington.edu/otap/).

in the decision-making process, even in the most patriarchal settings.

I wrote the final stages of this book at Duke University and the University of North Carolina at Chapel Hill in a peaceful and supportive environment. I am grateful to Erdağ Göknar and Nadia Yaqub for offering me the opportunity to be part of a vibrant intellectual community. Among many collaborations, I have had the pleasure of team-teaching a class with miriam cooke where we explored comparative ground for Arab, Persian, Hebrew, and Turkish writings by women. miriam has also read the early versions of this book and offered her invaluable feedback. Along with Erdağ and miriam, Bruce Lawrence, Sean Swanick, Zeina Halabi, and Banu Gökarınksel have given me insight during delicious *sohbets* (conversations).

During the years I have worked on this book, I received generous support from the Institute of Turkish Studies, a Research Grant for Faculty at the University of Utah, and a Research Grant for Faculty at Duke University. The librarians at the Topkapı Palace Museum, Istanbul University Library, and Fatih Millet Library have also been particularly helpful with the visuals in this book.

I have been fortunate to have two efficient editors. Suzanne Guiod at Syracuse University Press has made the process smooth and exciting. The anonymous readers were carefully selected and their reports helped transform this book. It was thanks to their expert comments and Suzanne's gentle encouragement to move forward that I was able to bring this project to its final state. Karly Alderfer has been on my side throughout the many versions and, with her diligent readings, she has helped me express my thoughts more clearly each time.

Some people enter our lives for a reason. Talat Halman was that person for me. When I first heard him reading couplets from Şeyh Galip in our class, I had no idea Ottoman poetry could be that beautiful. Talat Hoca, with his passion for Ottoman as well as English and American literatures, was the reason I began studying Ottoman literature. It does not do justice to call him an inspiration. Meeting him and being his student were life-changing events.

There are no distinctions between colleagues and family when you live with a project for more than a decade. Regardless of their profession and sometimes before they are even aware, they get involved in the process. My mother shared my passion for women writers and Mihrî. She was my companion during many trips to manuscript libraries and, most importantly, during my trip to Amasya. Over the course of a few weeks, we walked around the city and tried to envision Mihrî's life many centuries ago. Likewise, my father has always read everything I have written. We had many disagreements, including heated debates, but also very affectionate discussions that always helped me examine my arguments from a fresh perspective.

My son Emre has grown up on campuses, always hearing about Ottoman history and Mihrî. There are challenges for a child who grows up with a mother who sometimes gets lost in her books and computer. I am deeply grateful for his presence, a constant reminder for me to step out of my books and back into life.

Last but not least, my brother Cüneyt, a brilliant software engineer but also my writing coach, editor, babysitter, cook, and best friend: none of this would be possible without his unconditional support. He has been the *hami* (patron) of this project from the beginning to the end. If more women had a brother like him, we would have more women writers.

A Note on Transliteration and Use of Original Terms

There is no universal standard for transliterating Ottoman Turkish into Latin script. In this book, for primary sources and proper names and titles, I have chosen to use common modern Turkish transliteration followed by the *Turkish Encyclopedia of Islam*. For Arabic and Persian words and titles, I have followed the guide suggested by the *International Journal of Middle East Studies*. Therefore, if I discuss Turkish *kaside* I used Turkish, whereas if I discuss Arabic *qasida* I used Arabic transliterations. For secondary sources, I have not changed the way they appear in respective documents. For frequently used terms, I used the original Ottoman Turkish versions, and at first appearance I included English translations in parentheses. If the terms occur repeatedly, I also included them in the glossary of terms.

Mihrî Hatun

Introduction

A Female Lion in a Male Arena

> How can one know the story of Mihrî, who has not read
> Her petition on the grief of your torment and cruelty[1]

Because there are so few recorded in early modern history, a woman poet's words easily induce curiosity, if not fascination. As Mihrî Hatun herself says in the above-mentioned lines, the only way to learn about her story is to read "her petition on the grief of [the beloved's] torment and cruelty," meaning her poetry. These lines are extracted from one of the poems in her divan, of which four manuscript copies remain intact.[2] What could an early modern Ottoman woman say about her life, ideas, and thoughts in her poems? Does the poetic language leave enough space for anyone—man or woman—to express anything about the reality of their lives? And what would that mean in the context of early modern history?

1. See appendix, poem no. 18.

2. The four manuscript copies of "Mihrî Hâtun Dîvanı" consulted for this book are located in Fatih Millet Library, National Library in Ankara, Süleymaniye Library in Istanbul, and Istanbul University Library. There are two critical editions of Mihrî's divan. The first is out of print and its commentary is in Russian (Mihrî Hatun 1967), and the second is in Turkish (Mihrî Hatun 2007).

This book tells the story of Mihrî primarily through using her writings as a reflection on what it means to be a woman vis-à-vis the male-dominant discourse in early modern Ottoman court culture. Her collection provides us with an exceptional vantage point in literary history, bringing into focus not only the life of a woman poet but also questions of gender in intellectual fields. It allows us to ponder mundane questions about the social and economic conditions that prepared for her existence in intellectual circles, as well as about the intellectual and aesthetic challenges she faced in a male-dominated field.

Contextualizing a woman poet and her writings within early modern Ottoman intellectual history is unusual. Traditionally, the history of ideas and knowledge production has focused on the writings of the male scholarly elite who trained in the religious or secular sciences in *medreses* (higher-education institutes in Islamic societies). Women were not allowed to study in *medreses*; therefore, presumably, they could not have been a part of this "high" intellectual life. Although there were influential women in Islamic history, women were not expected to be scholars.[3] I will address this issue later in this chapter. For now, I would like to point out that, thanks to recent scholarship that has reevaluated different forms of education or writings of individuals from all walks of life (e.g., Sufi diaries and dream chronicles) as part of intellectual history, we now know that knowledge production was not confined to this very small group of elites (Kafadar 1994; Niyazioğlu

3. Leila Ahmed (1992, 99) mentions several women who have influenced Islamic religious thought. Some are well known, such as the Prophet's wife Aisha or Rabi'a al-Adawiyya, and others less so, such as the two women teachers of al-Ghazali (1165–1240); Shams, the mother of the poor; and Nunah bint al-Muthanna.

2016). These "soft" documents not only allow us to incorporate underrepresented groups in the major histories, but they have shown us that sometimes even the sultan himself preferred to write poetry or register his dreams rather than compose scholarly works (Felek 2014). This book is a contribution to the growing scholarship that uses different narrative genres to grasp the history of knowledge by introducing not only a discussion on women's writing but also the ideas and concepts of gender and sexuality.

Mihrî, like many intellectuals and artists of her time, composed poetry. Her poems reflect her social, political, and economic conditions, but they also discuss the concepts of gender in Ottoman court culture. However, traditional scholarship has considered early modern poetry to be a highly stylized form that had no relation to reality. Fedwa Malti-Douglas, for instance, chose to focus on prose in her revolutionary work, *Woman's Body, Woman's Word* (1992), in which she challenged many boundaries, such as chronologic approaches to history, and investigated the intersections in the Arabic canon to define a discourse of Arab women. Malti-Douglas (1992, 4) explains that "prose by its nature permits clearer representation, a more elaborate reformulation and restructuring of the world. Mimesis is tied to its essence."

The idea of mimesis may differ in Islamic aesthetics from the Western meaning. As Jamal Elias (2012, 28) discusses, the forms of representation in the Islamic arts correspond through systems of signification: "A 'representation' is superior (or perhaps more powerful) to that which it represents in some important aspects." He continues, "[R]esemblance is not a matter of 'looking like' something (with the photograph of a known person being the most accurately representative), but rather of perfectly embodying those aspects of the relationship of representation" (30). In other words, the kind of representation that can be found in Islamic art, or in poetry for the purposes of this book, can be a series of signifying processes rather than the simple enumeration of dates and times. One good example is the chronogram genre, which registers dates through the numeric values of letters rather than by numbers themselves. Recent studies on Ottoman poetry have also shown that poetry is a complex signifying system: it functions in various ways when we look at how the different discourses are established for each genre and how poets used them for their purposes and for certain occasions (Andrews and Kalpaklı 2005). On a related note, some poets clearly spell out names and places that had real-life values (Kuru 2006). Depending on the way it is read, poetry can reflect real life.

Mihrî drew considerable attention in her time and continues to do so today. Despite being a clear challenge to the norms, she was acclaimed and accepted as a good poet in intellectual circles. Among more than four hundred male poets, she was one of three women poets mentioned in the first *tezkires* of the sixteenth century. Although the *tezkire* tradition would continue to develop and expand throughout Ottoman history, another three hundred years or so would pass before they would mention any other women poets. The curious inclusion of women in the sixteenth-century *tezkires* is explained by Selim Kuru as related to the development of the Ottoman *tezkire* tradition itself. Kuru proposes that, by the end of the 1500s, the practice of poetry had witnessed considerable change, as poets were having more difficulty finding patrons than in earlier times. He connects this change with the ongoing process of centralization in the Ottoman Empire (Kuru 2000, 1–20). In other words, the emergence of the *tezkire* tradition in the sixteenth century coincided with a turning point in Ottoman history. These biographical dictionaries brought together early and contemporary poets under the same umbrella, which could be seen as a statement of "Ottomanness" against the prevalence of Arabic and Persian intellectuals. Moreover, by compiling and recording poets' biographies, *tezkire* writers began the construction of the Ottoman literary history. Including a few women poets in that history, however, is a curious detail that I discuss in part 1 of this book. I argue that women's entrance into the field as new actors is comparable to women's experience in the nineteenth century, when women were celebrated by the modernist male writers. For this reason, among others, this book joins the scholarship that has chosen the term "early modern" over medieval or premodern to define the sixteenth century.[4]

At this point, I think it is necessary to explain how I use gendered categories such as "woman," "man," and "male-dominated" in this book. While considering the gender matrix of the courtly discourse from the perspective of a woman requires an initial strategic essentialism—because she is defined as "a woman" in the major histories—my discussion will evolve and highlight the fluidity of gender categories in this period. The gender of an Ottoman woman poet is fundamentally related to the Ottoman literary tradition and its

4. I use the term "early modern" throughout this book to refer to the period from approximately the end of the fifteenth through the seventeenth centuries. The reason for using early modern instead of "medieval" is that medieval connotes backwardness. This period in Ottoman literary history represents the early stages of an enlightenment in terms of developments, particularly in arts and literature. It is in this period that poets such Ahmed Paşa, Ahmed-i Dâî, Necâtî Bey, Revânî, and Tâcîzâde Cafer Çelebi composed the poetry that later became canon, and the *tezkires* compiled hundreds of artists and poets reflecting a vibrant courtly culture. Early modern is an apt term for this study because Mihrî Hatun emerges as a gender-conscious woman. For other studies using the term "early modern," see Andrews and Kalpaklı 2005, Goffman 2002, and Zilfi 1997.

gender construction. Without keeping this in mind, it is possible to fall into the traps of generalization and marginalization. Although Mihrî Hatun's text does raise questions of gender, it would be tempting but naïve to consider her a representative of all Ottoman women. It is impossible to make such a claim because we do not have enough documentary evidence.

Cemal Kafadar outlines issues that might arise in research focusing on women in Ottoman history in a threefold manner. First, "Ottoman women" is a problematically broad category, encompassing different regions, ethnic and religious backgrounds, and social classes. Great detail is lost through such an approach (Kafadar 1993, 192). Second, the tendency to look at the Ottoman past from the stance of the present often reduces and simplifies issues despite considerable change and complexity over the centuries. Third, the consideration of "women" as a single and separate category from men places women in a marginalized position. Although I agree with the first two issues Kafadar raises, this book also shows how a strategic essentialism is, to some extent, necessary when women are systematically dismissed from the intellectual fields on the basis of gender alone. The ratio of men to women in *tezkires* is the reason for the male-dominant nature of intellectual circles. It does not mean, however, that this group is necessarily masculine or feminine, or that it had any fixed gender values.

Since Simone de Beauvoir ([1949] 1993, 283) first suggested in her magnum opus *The Second Sex* that "one is not born, but rather becomes, a woman," "woman" as a category has been seen within feminist theory as a construction of patriarchal ideologies, rather than relating to nature or biological factors. Building on de Beauvoir, this book makes use of three major concepts: Julia Kristeva's "subject position" and "marginality" as well as Judith Butler's "performativity." According to Kristevan identity politics, gender is a position of subjectivity that is bound with language (Kristeva 1984). It is present before and after the person who identifies with the relative gender. Drawing on Lacanian psychoanalysis, Kristeva asserts that becoming a subject is an awareness constructed through language. The meanings attached to "I" preexists the subject and, by owning it, the person embodies the qualities attached to it. "I" is male, "I" is white, "I" is black, "I" is beautiful. For Kristeva, there is no essential or biological subjectivity; there are only positions. Therefore, it is possible to resist and challenge them by simply taking alternative subject positions.

Drawing on her semiotic politics, Kristeva explains the unique position of the marginal, who is outside this symbolic order. She privileges the marginal as it has the potential to initiate a revolt in the narrative of the order. She includes marginalized woman as having the potential to cause a rupture in the narrative language, specifically because the discourse does not give her a subject position, that is, agency to express herself. Marginalized subjects have the advantage of not belonging to the center; thus, they have the freedom of not abiding by its laws. By being the "other," they also help define the center. In their position of being a necessary part of this order, they are the only ones who can transcend it. Kristevan marginality can initiate a certain kind of subversion in power and meaning.

In this framework, when Mihrî composes poetry, her subject position is assigned as a "woman" who is not supposed to speak. She can only speak from the subject position of a woman in Ottoman poetic discourse, which happens to be a marginal one. Instead of pretending to be from the center—that is, disguising herself behind a male pseudonym—she challenged the dominant discourse from her subject position with its force of marginality. To do that, she had to confront both the qualities of a woman and a poet. The subversion happens as she proposes a new subject position: a woman poet, or a woman subject who speaks. When Mihrî speaks as a woman she causes a rupture in the poetic discourse. Her revolutionary potential stems from the fact that women are not included in the discourse of love; instead, all gendered values, masculine or feminine, are performed by men. A male poet could represent himself as the manly warrior of the battlefield of poetry and at other times he could play the role of the meek lover who is looking for the mercy of the beloved. Later in the book I will discuss how all of these gender roles in the poetic discourse were reserved for men.

Judith Butler's *Gender Trouble* transformed the field of feminist and gender theory with the suggestion that it is not just the category of "woman," but all genders that are socially constructed. Furthermore, neither "man" nor "woman" is or can be a universal category (Butler 1990, 24–25). Butler's concept of the performativity of gender acknowledges a historical process of a series of stylized acts. Through the execution of these stylized acts, gender is actualized in a specific context. These acts are continuously reproduced in different spaces in relation to one another. In other words, gender categories produce each other and are only meaningful in relation to one another, as well as in the context of variables such as time and place. Through repetition and reiteration, certain values of gender are established, but they can always be contested with subversive actions such as parody.

Based on her research on early modern European women writers, Ann Rosalind Jones discusses the significance of studying women poets, though they are few in number, as influential for our understanding of gender in history. She suggests that women poets should be analyzed in comparison to their male contemporaries, with and against the "male-defined discourses" of their time (Jones 1990, 8). Jones (1986,

299) asserts that, if women presented any challenge to the male-centered discourse, they did so by simply being poets and writing love lyrics at a time when women were discouraged from speaking about anything besides religion. It was not uncommon for women to write religious poems. However, the discourse of love, such as neo-Platonism or Petrarchism, centralizes sociosexual differences unlike any other literary mode (Jones 1990, 7). In the humanist early Renaissance society, the love lyric was the most prestigious and private genre, as opposed to the public-oriented epic or tragedy. But, as Jones (1990, 8) indicates, "in practice, however, the ideological matrix that associated open speech with open sexuality in women made love poetry an especially transgressive genre for them, the genre of a semiprivate sphere that broke down secure categories. The woman poet, exposing desire for a man who was not her husband to the gaze of a mass readership, was a public woman—a term that in the sixteenth century meant a whore." Consequently, a woman who dared to write love lyrics risked, at the very least, suspicion and gossip. As I will show in later chapters, suspicion and gossip about Mihrî Hatun were quite pervasive. At the same time, by writing poetry, she presented a challenge to the male-centered love discourse and its gender construction. The few women who did so managed not only to create a new space for themselves, but also to gain a reputation among audiences of both men and women.

❀

Within the relevant scholarship, there have been attempts to explain the existence of Mihrî and other Ottoman women poets within the literary history. Among studies on Ottoman women poets, such as those by Mübeccel Kızıltan (1994) or Nazan Bekiroğlu (1999), there is a tendency to compose historical surveys of women poets in article-length works, without an in-depth and/or comparative analysis of their works. These articles have mainly dealt with the question of whether women poets wrote differently. They assume the presence of a feminine as opposed to a masculine voice. Without much discussion, most of their suggestions go no further than speculating that some women poets had a feminine voice, Mihrî being chief among them. Her lines are frequently quoted, especially those that clearly express her desire for a male beloved, to suggest that she not only defended her gender, but also had supposed love affairs with men. Although these are accurate points, they cannot be evidence of her feminine voice. The main problem here is that masculinity and femininity are not innate qualities but modern binary constructions that may or may not fit with early modern Ottoman aesthetics.[5] As a result of their uncritical treatment of masculinity and femininity and their assignment to respective male and female bodies, these suggestions remain speculation and, more importantly, anachronisms.

Similarly, Mehmet Arslan, who published the critical edition of Mihrî's divan, suggests that Mihrî used both a feminine and masculine voice but does not critically consider these terms (Mihrî Hatun 2007, 81–89). Conversely, Kemal Silay attempts to answer the question by applying feminist theories of women's writing. Silay (1997) suggests that, rather than being feminine or masculine, women poets were unable to generate a female poetic tradition in premodern times. He argues that "upper-class Ottoman women who wanted to become classical poets had to find other ways of acceptance,

5. One good example is Annemarie Schimmel's (1997) book, *My Soul Is a Woman: The Feminine in Islam*, in which she surveys the meaning of being a woman and the feminine in spiritual literature and points to the changing concepts of femininity and masculinity throughout history.

and for this they had to negotiate a clever way" (213). However, he defines this "clever way" as an appropriation of the male poet's style of writing and "singing his words." Simply stated, Silay asserts that women could not go beyond imitating their male colleagues. In classical poetry, indeed, everyone imitated everyone else. Thus, the question is not really a matter of imitation, but rather alternative speaking positions. To conceptualize a woman's voice, it is necessary to look more closely at the poetic tradition and what happens when a woman speaks. In a tradition in which both the speaker/lover and the beloved are almost always male and their gender ambiguous, there seems to be no place for a woman. However, as Mihrî's poetry demonstrates, the gender ambiguity in the poetic discourse helps her define a new love construction: a woman lover and a male beloved.

Among the studies of Ottoman women poets, Zehra Toska's (2006) work asks critical questions about the possible reasons behind an elite woman's success in composing poetry in early modern times. Toska points out the possibility that Ottoman poetics, with their unique treatment of gender roles, allowed women poets to compose poetry without overstepping the genre's core values. Her discussion of the complexity of gender roles in the Ottoman poetic tradition shows that an investigation of gender construction in the Ottoman poetic tradition is a necessary step toward understanding a woman poet's work. What it means to be a man or a woman and the values of femininity and masculinity must be investigated within the tradition with which the woman poet engaged. In other words, the gender of the speaker is not essential; rather, it is contextual and it might be different than what we assume.

Besides these surveys on Ottoman women poets, Walter Andrews and Mehmet Kalpaklı's critical reading of *tezkire* entries on early modern women poets is an instrumental contribution for any discussion of women poets or gender construction in Ottoman poetry. All works mentioned thus far have used *tezkires* as their sole basis for biographical information without any critical analysis. Consequently, *tezkire* entries about women poets have been accepted as truth. Andrews and Kalpaklı, on the other hand, put them under close investigation to highlight the value judgments and inconsistencies in their narratives. Instead of offering more speculative suggestions, their analysis focuses on male poets' understanding of gender construction in poetry and how it influenced the way in which we understand women's existence in literature. Because their work has been a guiding force for this book, I begin the discussion from where they left off and complement it with a close analysis of Mihrî's poetry (Andrews and Kalpaklı 2005).

In light of what has been said about Mihrî, this book proposes a new approach for analyzing an early modern woman poet in terms of her place in the intellectual discourse. Rather than automatically interpreting her voice as "feminine" or an "imitation" because she is a woman, I try to contextualize her writing as part of a discursive practice that has its own constructions of gender.

Women in Early Modern Times

Apart from the complications of gender in the poetic discourse, what was it like for a woman who aspired to participate in intellectual endeavors during Mihrî's time? Women in European and Islamic contexts had to transcend social boundaries to achieve this goal. In both contexts, it was exceptional for a woman to take part in intellectual circles, and the obstacles such a woman would have faced would have been similar. The first obstacle, as I mentioned briefly above, is the issue of education (a pervasive issue for women throughout history). In *A Room of One's Own*, Virginia Woolf writes about how women being denied access to the intellectual world has been an ongoing issue from Shakespeare's time until the twentieth century. Her pseudofictional character who could only enter the university library with the guidance of a male usher is a parody of this situation (Woolf [1929] 2012, 6). Woolf was herself educated at home, as women were not allowed access to institutional education in England. The privileged class would often educate their girls at home and, to some extent, this was not necessarily a disadvantage. Ann Rosalind Jones (1990, 6) highlights the issue of education when discussing Louise Labé, the French Renaissance poet, and her call for women "to study and to write in order to prove the injustice of men's denying access to education to an equally capable sex."

Although institutionalized education seems to be a universal obstacle for women, a close look at Islamic history will reveal that Islamic scholars found nothing fundamentally wrong with women's education. Based on *hadith* (the sayings or actions attributed to the Prophet Muhammad) and *sunna* (custom or practices of the Prophet Muhammad contained in the *hadith*), the Ottoman Islamic scholar Kınalızâde Âlî Çelebi (2012, 372) suggested that both boys and girls should be trained according to their nature. He quotes the following *hadith* as an example: "Both Muslim men and women should study [sciences]" (224). Kınalızâde Âlî Çelebi's work is a good example of *adab* (code of conduct) books, which were used for educating boys and girls. Annemarie Schimmel (1997, 11) emphasizes the significance of *adab* books in girls' education as "edifying guides for young girls that describe the proper deportment of women" in Islamic culture. These books exist in almost all languages spoken by Muslims, and they serve as guides about the ideals to which good Muslim men and women should aspire. In terms of primary education in Islamic societies, *sıbyan mektepleri* (primary schools) in Ottoman towns were established by religious foundations and were open to both girls and boys (Faroqhi 2000, 186). As Leila Ahmed (1992, 113) reports, there were similar schools in the Arab world called *kuttabs*, which boys and girls attended to receive primary education.

Although discussions about the possibility of educating girls in Islamic societies are helpful, it is necessary to define the type of education. Apart from the well-known institutionalized education in *medreses* (higher-education schools for men), there were other types of education. As Jonathan Berkey (1992, 96) discusses, the *medrese* system was only there to educate men to be the scholars who had the authority to "discharge certain religious and legal duties." There were also much larger, informal systems like the master and apprenticeship in Sufi convents or any kind of training for craftsmanship (e.g., poetry). This type of education, particularly in the urban centers, was open to anyone outside of the educated elite. As Berkey suggests, women might have benefited from this system. In terms of becoming a poet, *medrese* education was not necessary; in fact, many celebrated poets in the early modern period such as Necâtî or Zâtî did not receive *medrese* education.

It is clear from the existence of women scholars in Islamic history that women could receive education. For instance, Ruth Roded (1994, 2) surveyed women in Islamic biographical dictionaries from the eighth century until the present and found that "[i]n many classical biographical dictionaries . . . from less than one percent to 23 percent of the entries were women." As time passed, Roded explains, less significant scholars were dropped and there were few illustrious women to replace them.

The established Syrian mystic and scholar of the sixteenth century, 'Ā'ishah al-Bā'ūnīyya (d. 1517) is a good example of an early modern woman intellectual who appears in several biographical dictionaries. As Homerin (2011, 7) reports, 'Ā'ishah received extensive education and mystical training, which can be seen in her poetry. Coming from a family of religious scholars, she was educated at home. She not only memorized the Qur'an at a very early age, but she also made her pilgrimage to Mecca and wrote both prose and poetry. According to Homerin (2011, 14–15), she pays constant tribute to her spiritual masters. Like 'Ā'ishah, Umm Hani Maryam (1376–1466) was an intellectual woman from Cairo who also memorized the Qur'an, made her pilgrimage to Mecca, and studied Islamic arts and sciences (Ahmed 1992, 106). According to Leila Ahmed (1992), Umm Hani Maryam lectured in *medreses* and gave out *ijazas* (diplomas) to her students. She was a master of calligraphy, grammar, poetry, history, and Islamic jurisprudence.

It was not impossible for women to study and practice the religious sciences in the early modern world. When it comes to artistic practices, though, women were almost invisible. Their invisibility likely can be explained by their lack of access to intellectual circles. In European and Islamic contexts, intellectual circles were gendered spaces that were dominated by men. In European and medieval Andalusian contexts, most representations of women were courtesans or slaves.[6] However, in the Ottoman and Persian contexts, they were elite women. Ann Rosalind Jones (1990, 3) explains the lack of women in intellectual fields with Gramsci's concept of hegemony and the give-and-take formulation: dominant powers

6. For a review of women poets in medieval Andalusia, see Segol 2009.

have to legitimate their authority through the consent of a less powerful group. For the educated male group to be dominant, they needed to prove their authority vis-à-vis the less educated women. Although all women poets in the Ottoman context were from the privileged class, Walter Andrews and Mehmet Kalpaklı (2005, 204), by appropriating Jones's formulation, find that the low number of women poets in early modern Ottoman literature shows the operation of patriarchies and their similarity in the Ottoman world and in Europe.

Apart from the similarities between women's lack of access to intellectual spaces in the Islamic and European cases, the reasons behind each case are significantly different. Jones explains that the prohibitions against women's public self-display further hindered their participation in literary practice. Likewise, Judith Brown and Robert Davis (1998, 1) point out that the awakening of men in renaissance Europe did not mean the same for women. Urban spaces were gendered and elite women were confined to private spaces. When elite women went out, which was rarely, they were surrounded by a group of servants. Studies of early modern European literature suggest that space was constructed as a dichotomy between public and private, the public being accessible only to men. Jones (1990, 2) claims that this kind of separation pushed women away from the literary scenes, whether through gentle persuasion or through threats and insults.

The idea of the public/private dichotomy as a hindrance to women's access to the intellectual milieu—and thus the printing press—in Europe does not explain women's lack of appearance in Islamicate literature. The public/private dichotomy does not clearly apply to early modern Islamic societies, as the "private" or interior was also "public": many functions usually associated with the public sphere in the European case were practiced in the interior in Islamicate societies. A good example of this is the mirroring relationship between the architectural layout of the Topkapı Palace and its political structure. The Ottoman state was governed by an intimate group of administrators from the interior courts. Leslie Peirce examines women's place in Ottoman politics by applying Bernard Lewis's argument about the horizontal power structure of Islamic societies—inside as powerful—as opposed to the vertical European power structures. In this frame, women of the imperial harem were not excluded from politics; on the contrary, they were in the middle of it. Peirce also reminds us that Turkish ruling states had always included women as active participants and that there was nothing new about women's participation in state business. What *was* new in the Ottoman administrative system around the early modern period was its increased centralization and religious focus. Peirce (1993, 271) suggests, "[t]he debate over women was thus not always about women; rather, they were often a metaphor for order." According to Peirce, these administrative changes initiated the unsympathetic discourse about women in politics.

Until the nineteenth century, Islamicate literature was performed in private spaces called *meclises* (gathering, either for social purposes or entertainment) and was primarily based on performance for an audience. Gaining access to a *meclis* could have been an issue for anybody, men or women. I do not mention this to undermine the added issue of gender. I do so, rather, as a way of indicating that a Western framework is not necessarily applicable to women's position in Islamicate intellectual space and that this issue necessitates further investigation. Moreover, the power relations around the European practice of publishing during this period were not pronounced within Islamicate literature. The difficulties, enumerated by Jones (1990), that a European woman writer faced when she wanted to publish her work would not have applied to an Ottoman or Persian woman. During this period, texts were handwritten and crafted by individuals. This means that women could have either written their own works (based on biographical dictionaries of calligraphers, we know that there were women calligraphers) or, if they had the means, simply pay male calligraphers to write anything they pleased (Kazan 2014).

Apart from physical access, women also had aesthetic limitations. In the pre-Islamic period, as Suzanne Stetkevych (2013) has claimed, women's elegies played a significant role in tribal living, inciting the men to fight for their people. Among these women poets was the well-known al-Khansa, who, on her conversion to Islam, was supported by Prophet Muhammad. She managed to adapt her poetry to the new Islamic system and, in this way, the blood laments of the Jahiliyya period survived in the new Islamic era. Besides elegies or religious poetry, women were not expected to produce love poems. As Ann Rosalind Jones (1990, 1) suggests, particularly within the genre of love poetry in Europe, "female silence was equated with chastity, female eloquence with promiscuity." Furthermore, during this period, the neo-Platonic codes of writing were constructed in a way that sidelined women.

Another difference between women poets of European and Islamicate literature is that, unlike most European women poets, Arab, Persian, and Turkish elite women did not feel the need to disguise either their names or their gender identities. Apart from a few examples, such as Pernette du Guillet and medieval troubadours, most of the early modern European women poets who wrote love poetry were courtesans.[7] Seen in

7. See Ann Rosalind Jones (1990) and Margaret Rosenthal's (1992) work on early modern women writers.

this light, the desire of the first Turkish woman novelist, Fatma Aliye Hanım (1862–1936), to hide her name when publishing her first translation in the nineteenth century (by signing her work as "an Ottoman woman") appears to be a modern phenomenon rather than a reflection of Islamicate practice. The early modern women poets in the Islamicate literature, who wrote poetry in all genres, came from elite families and did not feel the need to hide their identities.

Thanks to recent studies, what we know about women poets in the early modern period is expanding. Consequently, we have discovered that there are clear parallels between Persian and Ottoman experiences. We see elite women write about everything, in all genres. According to Sunil Sharma (2009), 'Awfī (d. 1221), the earliest Persian *tezkire* writer, lists only one woman poet, Rabe'a of Qozdar, known generally as a great mystic. However, based on 'Awfī's presentation of her, Sharma (2009, 147) suggests that she was originally a poet who was then later transformed into a charismatic mystic by Sufi writers such as Attar and Jâmî. Sharma's discovery is quite interesting. It confirms the similarities between a poet and a mystic in this period, as the discourse of love was constructed on the basis of neo-Platonic ideals. As Sharma describes, *Javāhir al-'Ajā'ib* (Jewels of Wonder) by Fakhri Haravī chronicles twenty women poets of the late Timurid period. Apparently, most of them lived under the patronage of Husayn Bayqara (d. 1506). Dawlatshāh and 'Alī Shīr Navā'ī also list women poets, Mahsati being the first example and Jahān Khātūn the most important (Sharma 2009, 147). Dominic Brookshaw's (2005, 174) work on Jahān Khātūn suggests that she came from the royal family, lived in Shiraz at the time of Hafez (d. 1389), and died sometime after 1393. Jahān Khātūn wrote in all genres, as can be seen in her published divan. Her 1413 *gazels*, as Brookshaw suggests, indicate that she performed in *meclises*. She herself held *meclises* in her palace, where the poets and intelligentsia of the time frequently met. 'Ubayd-i Zākānī's rather critical portrayal of Jahān Khātūn, who he describes as a woman who claimed to be a poet but did not have talent, is contradicted by Dawlatshāh, who praises her poems and characterizes her as a "refined woman" (Brookshaw 2005, 174).

Neither a woman poet's existence in literary circles nor attacks on her gender, aiming to push her to the margins, are unusual, as will be discussed in Mihrî's biographical story in the next chapter. Jahān Khātūn is a perfect example of an active royal woman. Similarly, the Mughal Princess Gülbadan (1523–1603), Emperor Babur's daughter, wrote a historical account of her brother Humayun's rule, entitled *Humayun-Nama* (Gülbadan 1944). Commissioned to write about the royal court by her nephew, her writing portrays a mixed *meclis*, one in which both elite women and men participated and recited their literary works (Szuppe 1996, 134).

Ottoman Women Poets

Regarding Ottoman literature, *tezkire* writers record three women poets in the sixteenth century, Mihrî being one of them.[8] These three women poets represent three different generations of Ottoman women during this period. Although the focus of this study is on Mihrî Hatun, the *tezkire* entries for the other two women poets, Zeynep Hatun and Ayşe Hubbî Hatun, shed light on the circumstances of women poets.

The first recorded Ottoman woman poet, Zeynep Hatun, lived before Mihrî and, according to Âşık Çelebi (2010, 591), was the daughter of a *kadı* (magistrate) in Amasya. Because of

8. For a survey of Ottoman women poets from the fifteenth to twentieth centuries, see Havlioğlu 2010a.

her father's support of her education, she learned Arabic and Persian languages and literature, became a talented musician, and wrote beautiful poetry. Unfortunately, other than a few lines mentioned in *tezkires*, her poetry has not survived. At some point, she married İshak Fehmi Efendi and gave up writing poetry, perhaps before Mihrî entered the literary circles of Amasya. As I describe later, many of the *tezkire* writers contrast Zeynep's choice to marry with Mihrî's choice to remain single—or, as they call her, a "virgin"—all her life.

Ayşe Hubbî Hatun (d. 1589–90), also born in Amasya, was active after Mihrî. She was the granddaughter of Akşemseddin, a prominent figure in Amasya, and the wife of Şemsi Çelebi, Selim II's teacher during his tenure as a *şehzâde* in Amasya. Later, Şemsi Çelebi served as a *şeyhülislâm* (head of religious matters). As a consequence of her marriage, Ayşe Hubbî entered the palace in Istanbul. She became a companion to Sultan Selim II and, later, to Sultan Murad III. Even after her husband's passing, she maintained her position at the palace. Ayşe Hubbî was well educated. She learned Arabic, studied poetry, and, according to *tezkire* writers, composed *mesnevîs* (narrative poems), *kasîdes* (odes), and *gazels* (lyric poems). Unfortunately, her poetry has not survived. Kızıltan (1994, 114) notes that her style was not "feminine" and that she wrote just like her male colleagues. She was praised in *tezkires* for her exceptional poetic skills, which exceeded those of her contemporaries in the Persian world, such as Jahān Khātūn.

According to Âşık Çelebi (2010) and the poet Cinânî, Ayşe Hubbî wrote a *mesnevî* entitled "Cemşîd ü Hurşîd," which has not survived. Müjgân Cunbur (1988) asserts that she also wrote a *risâle* (treatise) entitled "İmâdu'l-Cihâd." In her reading of this poem, signed "Hubbî," Cunbur explains that it discusses the topic of religious warfare and was written following a tradition of praising *gazâ* (a military expedition on behalf of Islam) and *gâzis* (soldiers who fight on behalf of Islam). Furthermore, the entire poem was composed with references to various *suras* (Qur'anic verses) and *hadiths* about the Prophet. If Ayşe Hubbî Hatun wrote this poem, as claimed by Cunbur, it shows that she had education in theology, had an interest in religious warfare, and composed poems on matters of political history.

Although there is no mention of specific names, in looking at the traces of poetry dedicated to women, we find that there must have been a prominent female presence, both as poets and patrons, in the palace during the time of Ayşe Hubbî Hatun. Nevertheless, most women were excluded from the pages of history. Apart from these three women poets, Mehmet Çavuşoğlu's coincidental discovery of a sixteenth-century woman poet, Nisâyî, in a *mecmua* (anthology), suggests that there were likely more women poets writing during this period, but that few were recorded. Çavuşoğlu (1978) claims that Nisâyî's elegy for Şehzâde Mustafa, who was executed by his father Süleyman I (1494–1566), was written in a very angry tone, which may be a reason for her exclusion from the *tezkires*. The following couplet is an example:

> You allowed the words of a Russian witch into your ears
> Deluded by tricks and deceit, you did the bidding of that
> spiteful hag
> You slaughtered that swaying cypress, fruit of life's orchard
> What has the compassionless Monarch of the World done
> to Sultan Mustafa? (Andrews and Kalpaklı 2005, 248)

In this couplet, Nisâyî refers to Hürrem Sultan (d. 1558) by her ethnicity, accusing Sultan Süleyman I and/or Rüstem Paşa (1500?–61), his grand vizier, of believing Hürrem Sultan's conspiracy against Süleyman's eldest son, Şehzâde Mustafa. Süleyman believed his wife's accusations against his son and had

Mustafa killed in 1553. Apparently, Mustafa was an important patron of poetry and the arts at his court in Amasya. Nisâyî was likely one of the many poets that gathered at his court and at that of his mother, Gülbahar Hatun. In other words, she was not on the side of the winner. In Çavuşoğlu's (1978) view, this is a good enough explanation for her disappearance from the pages of major historical texts. However, he also adds that Nisâyî's poetry has some serious faults of form. For that reason, she might not have been considered as qualified as the other three women poets, Zeynep, Mihrî, and Ayşe Hubbî. Although one might think that Nisâyî's criticism was the reason for her exclusion from the pages of history, other poets, such as Yahyâ Bey (d. 1582), also wrote elegies for Şehzâde Mustafa and criticized Sultan Süleyman I and Rüstem Paşa. Although they suffered the consequences, they remained recognized poets in Ottoman history.

It is interesting to note that Nisâyî was also from Amasya; Şehzâde Mustafa was the last prince-governor to be based there. Therefore, all known early modern Ottoman women poets, whether mentioned in *tezkires* or not, were from Amasya. This is a curious detail that raises questions about Amasya's significance as an urban center in the early modern Ottoman era—questions that I address later in my discussion of Mihrî's hometown.

Images of Women in Intellectual Circles

The historical presence of women poets in the early modern period suggest that they could compose poetry and be recognized for their works. Besides spatial challenges, they also had to work against the unfavorable images of "woman" in intellectual discourse. Apart from pure female figures that appear in the Qur'an such as Aisha, Zeyneb, or Fatima, the archetype of the female storyteller in literature as Scheherazade had both positive and negative connotations. Although some scholars do not include *1001 Nights* under the rubric of Islamicate literature, despite the existence of manuscripts in Arabic, Persian, Turkish, and Urdu, her character has had a significant impact on the way women are sexually scripted in both Islamicate and European literature. Scheherazade, the mother of storytelling, saves her own life and those of other women by telling a story every night. By doing so, she also cures the ailing King Shahryar. Meanwhile, the desire the king feels for her body is equal to that which he feels for her words—both of which were trapped in his bedroom. As Fedwa Malti-Douglas (1992, 11–29) suggests, Scheherazade is aware of this situation and her power emanates from being able to control his desire. However, in later texts, her success causes both admiration and suspicion of women.

As Afsaneh Najmabadi notes (1999, 203), the classical motif of the "cunning woman" who is comparable to Scheherazade is pervasive in Islamicate literatures. According to Malti-Douglas (1992, 11), the Arabo-Islamic discourse on women has its roots in the image of Scheherazade and continues to influence perceptions of today's Arab women writers. Malti-Douglas reminds us that some modern perspectives consider Scheherazade to be a cunning woman who plays "tricks" on—or seduces—her audience with her words, this being the reason for her success. One of these "tricks" is telling fantastic stories that amuse the king and change the perspective of the most powerful man in the country.

Afsaneh Najmabadi and Gayane Karen Merguerian (1997) discuss another active female character in Islamicate and other Middle Eastern literature: Züleyhâ, one of the two main characters of the classic Yusuf and Züleyhâ story. In the versions of the story of Yusuf in the Qur'an and the Old Testament, the name Züleyhâ does not appear; rather, she is called simply "Aziz's wife" in the Qur'an or "Potiphar's wife" in the Judeo-Christian tradition. However, this story was retold many times in Arabic, Judeo-Arabic, Persian, and Ottoman languages, and it evolved into a love story between Yusuf and "Aziz's wife." In these literary versions, "Aziz's wife" gains a name: Züleyhâ. She is an active lover who pursues Yusuf, the beloved. In other words, literary versions of the story make Züleyhâ the main character of the love story. As Najmabadi and Merguerian (1997) note, it is, perhaps, for this reason that some find it inappropriate for girls to read stories of Yusuf and Züleyhâ.

In early modern times, it was a common literary tool for poets to identify themselves with classical characters, such as Mecnûn or Ferhâd, and to describe the beloved as Leylâ, Şîrin, or Yusuf. Unsurprisingly, I have not encountered any early modern male poet who specifically identified with the character of Züleyhâ. Only female poets, beginning with Mihrî Hatun, specifically identify themselves with Züleyhâ. This identification is understandable: Züleyhâ is one of the only examples of a female lover, although she is not viewed favorably in the religious narratives. However, her character underwent a narrative transformation in mystical literatures. Beginning with Jâmî's story of Yusuf and Züleyhâ, she is remade into an ideal lover.

The topos of cunning women and women's magic or tricks is pervasive throughout early modern literary history in both Islamicate and European cases. There are several examples of women's "witchcraft" in European literature. One such example is Veronica Franco's inquisition trial on accusations of witchcraft, a reaction to her success in writing and her manipulation of power relations. As Rosenthal (1992, 153) discusses, Franco managed to turn her defense into a literary performance, thus saving herself. The suspicion of a woman's success in intellectual pursuits or in gaining political clout was translated into representations of these women as dangerous and mysterious. A good example of such discourse is discussed by Kathryn Babayan in her treatment of an early modern Persian text entitled *ʿAqāʾid al-Nisā* (Beliefs of Women) by Aqā Jamāl Khwānsārī, a cleric. The work focuses on the daily activities of women in seventeenth-century Isfahan, mainly discussing five female characters, all of whom were superstitious (Babayan 1998, 351). As she critically reevaluates the author's ridicule of his subjects, Babayan points out that this work holds valuable information about women's daily lives at the time. For instance, the text relates that women were able to go out and socialize among themselves in the marketplace or bathhouses, although it also uses some of these facts to demonize them. Babayan suggests that we can read the fundamental changes occurring at that time within the administrative system of the Safevid Empire as an explanation for the misogynistic works produced in this period.

The misconceptions about women found in intellectual discourses appear to have been a major obstacle for a woman who aspired to produce within the permissible limits of the tradition. The strategies they used to survive within the discourse were often interpreted as tricks. The survival of a woman poet in the male-dominated intellectual world can be metaphorically compared to Scheherazade's own survival. Her power originates from her understanding of her audience's perspective of her gender and her ability to control this perspective. She does not resist being a "woman"; on the contrary, she claims it. Sometimes through claiming this role with a new performance, sometimes through parody, she subverts its meaning by highlighting the superficiality of the way in which the concept of the "woman" is constructed.

Women writers in the early modern world had to overcome obstacles that are not obvious from today's perspective.

Considering the performative nature of intellectual spaces, their major difficulty was to insert themselves as legitimate actors in physical and aesthetic spaces. This book will focus on these two obstacles: the *meclis* culture and the poetic discourse as places of resistance for Mihrî to both perform and subvert from within. To move beyond speculations and develop an approach to Mihrî's life and work, it engages with her poetry alongside a variety of other texts, such as writings by her male contemporaries and secondary sources. A woman poet composing love poems—rather than religious poems—in a physically and aesthetically male-dominated field, poses an opportunity to reevaluate what we know about women in early modern times.

Mihrî Hatun's historical, sociopolitical, economic, and religious background contributed to the making of her persona. Therefore, any attempt to give meaning to her poetry that does not take her gender into consideration would be far from complete. For her biographers, she was first a woman, then a poet. Finally, a woman poet and her representation of gender in her poetry offers a new perspective on the courtly practice of the time, in particular the discourse of love.

This book is organized as an attempt to answer two major questions: first, what circumstances allowed for Mihrî's existence as a woman in the intellectual circles? Second, how did she carve herself a legitimate space in the aesthetic discourse?

Part 1, while focusing on the biography of Mihrî, tries to situate her in the *meclis* culture of the early modern Ottoman times. To assemble the biographical story of an early modern woman poet, it is first necessary to critically examine the existing sources and, more importantly, how these sources identify and discuss a woman poet. In other words, I will try to define the discourse that constructs a way of conceptualizing women in the courtly culture. Following this, the discussion focuses on the important components of her career. The *meclis* practice might seem to have been a hindrance for women, but this section speculates on the possible advantages of this tradition for women. Because poetry was not written but performed, the space has a fundamental influence on the production of poetry and vice versa. In this framework, gender, among other things, is also constructed through a systematic and historical practice. Therefore, Mihrî's beloved city Amasya and Bayezid's patronage are important components of her social background. From the perspective of space, the goal is to situate the woman poet within her socioeconomic circumstances. When considering Mihrî in her time and place, there are a few points that stand out. First, because the intellectual and artistic fields were primarily dominated by men, a woman was marginal not only because of the overwhelming number of male artists, but also in terms of aesthetic values. Her marginality can clearly be noted in the male *tezkire* writers' discourse—which I define as "erotically humorous"—that was developed to discuss women and gender. It reflects norms, ideals, and value judgments. Another, subtler place in which she was marginalized was the aesthetic discourse of Ottoman poetry, which sidelined, if not degraded, her gender. In this aesthetic system, as a woman, she was supposed to be ignorant and silent.

Part 2 focuses on Mihrî's writing as both a legitimate and subversive act. In this section I primarily discuss the aesthetic obstacles she had to tackle, such as the discourse of love, and her subversive manner of overcoming these so as to carve out a legitimate place in the court culture. Although it was marginal in the male-dominated literary tradition, Mihrî was very clear about her gender and was not apologetic about it. To highlight the specific maneuvers in her writing, I discuss poetic dialogues between her and two male contemporaries: Necâtî (1451–1509) and Makâmî (dates unknown). Through a comparative analysis, I try to identify Mihrî's personal choices in composing her poetry and competing with her male peers, such as challenging manliness as a male quality, her self-representation as Züleyhâ, and her use of humor to parody gender roles in the poetic tradition. In short, this section examines her alternative subject position: using traditional tools that, in her poetry, function as sites of resistance. Finally, in this part I argue that, although her performance as a poet challenged the poetic discourse and its gender structure, it remained within the permissible limits. Thus, her poetry was seen as legitimate and this is exactly why she survived.

Because one of the major suggestions of this book is that women's writing in Turkish might have a long history, the closing chapter discusses the possibility of applying the findings to a nineteenth-century case. Based on the idea of fluidity and continuity of history, the comparative case of Mihrî and Fatma Aliye is an experiment in highlighting the patterns of women's writing as a tradition in history.

PART ONE

Mihrî Hatun

The Making of a Woman Poet

1. A female courtier holding a flower and a book. Detail, Topkapı Palace Museum Library, B. 408, "Album of I. Ahmed" (seventeenth century), fol. 8b.

1

A Lucky Star Is Born

Having reached the water of life, Mihrî will not die 'til
the Resurrection
Because she saw İskender clearly in the darkness of night[1]

She opened her eyes from sleep and there he was, a shining moonlit face. "O you, love thief!" she thought to herself. "Are you my lucky star? My Jupiter, maybe?" It was as if her ordinary room had been turned into the evening sky and he was the illuminating star. With that beautiful face, he must be a Muslim. But with that sheet around him he looked like a trouble-making infidel. "No, this can't be true," she mumbled. She couldn't be so lucky as to have him here. So, she closed and opened her eyes again. And he was gone! Like an angel, he disappeared into the unknown. She realized, then, that of course she was lucky. Because even the single moment that she saw him was enough. She felt as if she was young and beautiful again. As if İskender helped her, like he did his friend Hızır, by showing her the way through the darkness to the fountain of life. From now on she would not die until the Judgment Day.

This paraphrasing of one of Mihrî Hatun's most famous poems tells the story of her waking up one night to the face of the beloved. She compares her ecstasy to reaching the fountain

1. See appendix, poem no. 12.

of youth, or immortality. As quoted above, in the poem's last couplet, she pronounces the beloved's name clearly: İskender. Her biographers' interest in this love story is not the only reason for its popularity. A closer look will reveal its aesthetic value. The blurry line between dreams and waking life, or between reality and imagination, is constructed, giving a sense of ambiguity necessary for layers of meaning.

Mihrî seems, on the one hand, to be talking elusively about a mysterious encounter with a man named İskender. Apparently, one night, she opens her eyes from sleep and sees him in front of her. She is struck by his beauty and cannot be sure whether he is real. To confirm, she closes and reopens her eyes but, when she does so, he disappears. She interprets this experience as a lucky incident because she was fortunate enough to see this vision of İskender. Alluding to the legend about İskender, she considers her experience comparable to drinking the water of life.

According to legend, İskender is a combination of Alexander the Great and the Qur'anic Zü'l-Karneyn (the man with two horns; see Qur'an, Sura XVIII, The Cave, verses 83–101). In addition to a brief Qur'anic parable, there is an expansive narrative based on this historical and religious character. After conquering the world, İskender was left with nowhere to lead his army except the land of darkness in the most distant East, where he hoped to find the water of life to gain immortality (for a detailed story, see Andrews, Kalpaklı, and Black 2006, 45–48). Alluding to the myth, Mihrî implies in her poem that, having seen a vision of him, she herself has reached immortality. In the literary world, the legendary İskender represents the inspiration that compels her to compose poetry, which will eventually make her immortal.

On the other hand, Mihrî could be referring to a real lover sleeping beside her, but instead she speaks in metaphorical terms, saying that she is in a dream because she cannot believe how lucky she is to have him. This interpretation is possible because she would not have been able to or wanted to speak openly about her love life. Though the tension between the opposing ideas of reality and dreams maintains a sense of suspense, the traditional reading of it suggests my first elaboration: a poet's imagined encounter with the legendary İskender. Regardless, her biographers purposefully refer to the literal option. For them, the poem is not speculative, but a reflection of reality. Their legitimation of this far-fetched interpretation is based on Mihrî's use of dreams, a common literary tool, to relate her story.

Within the Islamicate aesthetic background, because of their prophetic relevance, dreams are considered signs from the other world, which was considered the true realm.[2] In Ottoman literary practice, dreams work as functional tools to explain and legitimate an important turning point; for example, Osman, the first Ottoman sultan, and his prominent dream as the beginning of the Ottoman state. Similarly, the Ottoman traveler Evliyâ Çelebi narrates his dream as an explanation for his excursions. In the same vein, poets used dreams as an excuse for writing/composing an artistic work (Gündüz 2009, 190). Overall, they not only represent inspiration but also a revelation of truth. In short, dreams help to explain the unexplainable and assign it spiritual value. They are accepted as a way to unravel hidden meanings, and they bring news from the other world. As Aslı Niyazioğlu (2010) argues, Âşık Çelebi, one of Mihrî's biographers, used dreams to explain the nature of incidents. Considering this function,

2. Jamal Elias (2012, 198–216) explains the process of seeing, telling, and interpreting a dream as a cultural practice in Islam.

biographers make assumptions about Mihrî's understandable choice of using a dream: it reveals her attempt to unravel a hidden truth that cannot be pronounced openly because it is not acceptable. An illicit love affair must have been considered transgressive. If she did not want to harm her reputation, she could only discuss it within the realm of a dream.

Thanks to the shields of the poetic world, we will never know if Mihrî was writing about a real person named İskender. Though the ambiguous nature of this type of poetry allows the reader/audience to assign desired meanings, the biographers' choice of an alternative and less common meaning is curious. As Selim Kuru suggests, it was not uncommon for a poet to pronounce the beloved's real name and to clearly refer to a worldly love.[3] Furthermore, the subsequent biographies of Mihrî Hatun and the gossip represented as reality pose significant questions about writing the life story of an early modern Ottoman woman. How much of her biography, as written in texts that have been accepted as historical documents, reflects the true realities of her everyday life? Was it possible to represent her true story?

The uncritical acceptance by Mihrî's biographers—and by those who subsequently wrote about her—of the far-fetched meaning of this poem points to a problematic yet prevailing narrative about Mihrî.[4] Like their insistence on her relationship with the so-called İskender, their accounts of her consist mostly of anecdotes. Although none of these biographers lived during the same time period as her and the information they present is all secondhand, *tezkires* have been considered

3. Selim Kuru (2007, 163) discusses poems with clear names.

4. Based on the *tezkires*, Şennur Sezer's (2005) docudrama of Mihrî's life has become a popular story about Mihrî Hatun.

documentary evidence in Ottoman literary studies. Consequently, everything we know about Mihrî today has been mostly based on the imagination of early modern male intellectuals. Our information about her is limited to their interest in a woman poet's life: her morality, marital status, virginity, and supposed love affairs, such as the one with the so-called İskender.

The usual categories employed to represent male poets in *tezkires*, such as information about their education or administrative positions that they held (i.e., basic biographical information), are not applicable for women.[5] When it comes to representing a woman, *tezkire* writers either reflect their own misconception of women or predict and speak to that of their audience. In their narratives, after setting up the suspicion of a love affair, they attempt to protect her respectability because, in the end, they need to explain the reason for including women in their work. Almost all of her biographers were eager to protect her chastity, though they did not refrain from providing details about a promiscuous love story. As Latîfî (2000, 510) wrote, while Mihrî was in love with İskender Çelebi, the son of Sinan Paşa, she wrote him several poems expressing her love for him but "she didn't bring his cypress [form] near [to her] and making his body resemble a bow, his ruby tipped-arrow could not strike its target."

Latîfî's narrative is a good example of a *tezkire* approach to describing Mihrî Hatun. While *tezkire* writers seem to protect her chastity, they also employ an erotic language to do so. Though it may look as if the biographers contradict themselves, I argue that their consistently sexually explicit narrative

5. For a focused discussion on the biographical details conveyed in *tezkires*, see Tolasa 1983.

serves their purpose of including women as desirable new members of poetry in the sixteenth century. To be included in the poetic circles, a poet is expected not only to be promiscuous but also to have an ambiguous gender. As this chapter focuses on Mihrî's biography, it first analyzes the narrative of *tezkires* as a necessary step toward unraveling what she represented in the intellectual circles. Despite what Mihrî achieved as a poet, for *tezkire* writers she was first and foremost a *woman* whose qualifications as a poet had to be confronted and reevaluated. A close analysis of their discourse will not only reveal the textuality and narrativity of their account of Mihrî—it will showcase the intimate language used among the intellectual circles. Only after such an inquiry is it possible to reconstruct her biographical story and understand her positioning in the early modern Ottoman literary space.

The Woman Poet as a Historical Process

As discussed in the previous chapter, the incongruity between women and secular literature in the early modern world has been an issue of debate in modern scholarship. Though love poetry was apparently a male business, we do come across a few women poets in literary history, particularly in Ottoman literary history. Walter Andrews and Mehmet Kalpaklı (2005, 197) wrote that it is surprising that, "given the erotic character of Ottoman poetry and what we now imagine the traditional protectiveness of Islam toward female virtue, is that there are any entries for women at all." Islamic intellectual history has always included women, and the Ottomans must have been familiar with female participation in knowledge production (Roded 1994). As for the matter of poetry, Andrews and Kalpaklı (2005, 203) add that, "by the rules of custom and tradition, a woman should not be exposed to public scrutiny as a poet necessarily is." What is apparent specifically in the sixteenth century is not the inclusion of women in intellectual history for the first time, but, as Andrews and Kalpaklı highlight, their surprising inclusion in an erotic milieu, which can be considered incongruous with our understanding of the Islamic past. In addition, unlike the case of the European courtesans, the Ottoman women poets were notable members of the elite class. They were included and acclaimed not only by their male contemporaries, but also by primary patrons, such as the sultan of that time.

Once women were included in the nonreligious literary scene, they were subject to eroticization and the scrutiny of their reputations. Apart from the complicated reasons for including women in their works, the erotic language *tezkire* writers used to present these women is in fact a type of initiation for them into the intimate circles. *Tezkire* writers' development of a discourse to present the desirable but still respectable woman, a female partner for the male poet in the game of literature, is curious yet has survived throughout the centuries. Considering the homosocial tradition of the early modern intellectual circles, it is not surprising that they employ a discourse that I have elsewhere defined as "erotically humorous" to speak about sexuality and gender (Havlioğlu 2015b; El-Rouayheb 2005).

Ottoman women's entrance into the literary scene coincides with a turning point in literary history, which can be defined as the "Ottomanization" of literature. They first appear in *tezkires*: massive collections that present and preserve poets that came into existence in the sixteenth century. *Tezkires* are thought to have evolved from the *ṭabaqat* system, an Arabic tradition in which biographical information was organized according to certain chronological categories. The first *tezkire* that compiled poets was written in Persian by Dawlatshāh (b. 'Ala' al-Dawla, 1431–95, with the title of

Tadhkirat al-shuʿarāʾ). The major role model for the Ottoman writers, however, was ʿAlī Shīr Navāʾī, who followed Dawlatshāh with his *tezkire* composed in Chagatai Turkish.[6] The first Ottoman *tezkire* writer, Sehî Bey (d. 1548), in his *Heşt Behişt* (Eight Heavens), explains that he wrote this work to prevent the included poets from being lost to time (Tolasa 1983, 63). His successors, Latîfî (d. 1582) and Âşık Çelebi (1519–71), followed him in this pursuit within the same century.

Besides the articulated need to record Ottoman poets, Sehî Bey and other *tezkire* writers made conscious choices as to what constituted a poet, what characteristics poetry should possess, and who should be included or excluded in their *tezkires.* They paid attention to the following details: first, the poet's identity, or their social, cultural, economic status and relationships, personal traits, and physical qualities; and second, his or her literary value, or their literary skills, education, and training, the poet's networking in intellectual circles, and the poet's work (Tolasa 1983, 80–81). In addition to creating the first canon of Ottoman literature, these biographers set the rules for traditions that, in time, developed into the poetics of Ottoman literature. Not only did they write the history of Ottoman literature, they also developed a critical perspective for this literary production, reflecting the value judgments of their time and intellectual milieu. Likewise, they simultaneously developed a structural and discursive model for including women in literary history.

Sehî Bey organized his work following the Persian model of Mawlanā Nūr al-Dīn ʿAbd al-Rahmān Jāmī's *Bahārestān* and Dawlatshāh's *tezkire.* He constructed his work in eight

6. Dominic Brookshaw (2005, 174) reports that there are twenty women poets registered in the *tezkire* of Dawlatshāh.

categories, which reflected the writers' social and educational status. For women poets, it also specified their gender.[7] In the subcategory entitled "zikrü'n-nisâ," or "mention of women," he explains the reasoning behind his inclusion of women poets.

> In this age there are two women poets. Because their poems are beautiful, their couplets are matchless, their gazels are popular, and their fame considerable, they have been included in this biographical collection. (Andrews and Kalpaklı 2005, 197; Sehî Bey 1978, 288–89)

By "two women poets," he meant Zeynep and Mihrî Hatun. The fact that he feels compelled to explain his reasons for including women implies the incongruity between women and intellectual fields. Therefore, Sehî Bey presents Zeynep and Mihrî as exceptional women. Because they composed exquisite poetry, their gender could be excused. He implicitly suggests that, through their poetry, they attained a gender role usually delegated only to men. Sehî Bey's categorization of women follows older traditions and norms for discussing women. For instance, in his *Nafahat al-Uns*, Jâmî also compiled women saints in a separate group. In both Arabic and Persian biographical dictionaries, women are introduced in similar ways.[8]

7. By "learned men," Sehî means men who had been educated in both religious and secular subjects. Halil İnalcık (2001, 173–86) explains that, according to Taşköprüzâde, Ottomans thought of knowledge as having four phases: spiritual, rational, verbal, and written. The disciplines that help to gain the knowledge of God or religion were considered primary, and the rest, such as astrology or logic, were secondary. Conversely, literary education meant working with masters, reading the poetry of predecessors and contemporaries, gaining familiarity with Islamicate canon, and writing *gazels* for practice with certain kinds of vocabulary and imagery.

8. For further discussion on the representation of women in biographical dictionaries, see Roded 1994.

In his brief entries on women poets, Sehî Bey does not elaborate beyond the basic information of their names and birthplaces, including short sections of their poetry. However, his successor Latîfî adds further information pertaining to Zeynep and Mihrî Hatun, using a very specific language. One of the major characteristics that sets Latîfî's *tezkire* apart from Jâmî's—or Sehî Bey's, for that matter—is his choice to organize his work alphabetically. By using an alphabetical system, Latîfî avoided stratifying the poets by social status or gender. Therefore, in Latîfî's work women poets are not as obviously marginalized through categorizations. However, by employing an erotically humorous discourse, he implicitly marginalizes them. In fact, he is the first *tezkire* writer to pay attention to Mihrî's body through her "femininity," "virginity," or "marital status." For instance, he compares her accomplishments in her poetry, such as *bikr-i mana* (untouched/untapped/new meanings), to her "virginity."

When the subject of conversation is "women" within the context of poetry, instead of factual information, *tezkire* writers find it appropriate to highlight gender first. Regardless of her profession, a woman's gender added "difference" to the categories applied to male poets. In other words, besides her other qualities as a poet, her gender was apparently her most distinct characteristic. In addition, a woman poet's marital status or supposed virginity were emphasized by including information about husbands, whereas some relevant information, such as her education, was left out. *Tezkire* writers briefly mention the men who influenced these women poets intellectually, such as their fathers or mentors. Their work is acknowledged as good and their collegiate relationship with other men is mentioned with caution—explained and excused with an emphasis on the necessity of such a relationship. The information provided on women poets is almost always much shorter than that for male poets. For instance, Mihrî's brief biography in the *tezkires* tells of a woman poet's career in relation to her male family members, male patrons, and male colleagues, the people *tezkire* writers knew. Her relations to the women in her family, or to women patrons, if there were indeed any, are left out. Consequently, it follows that the *tezkire* writers' representations of Mihrî were naturally biased by their male gender and their limited access to or interest in women's lives.

Through such careful organization, *tezkires* set the expected gender of the poet as men. The project of the Ottomanization of literature in the *tezkires* meant the self-construction of the early modern Ottoman literati through many textual maneuvers, including the production of the male poet and his lesser counterpart: the woman poet. They introduce this alluring new colleague, the woman poet, into the literary field with a dose of eroticism in an effort to legitimate her existence. At the same time, because these were respectable women, the writers counterbalance this intimate language with an emphasis on marital status or virginity to protect the women poets' reputations. They predict their audience's questions about the reputation of the women poets. The outcome is a curious representation of gender through a highly stylized language, which reflects the ambiguous nature of poetic values.

Latîfî and Âşık Çelebi present Mihrî Hatun as a woman, but because of her skills in poetry, they also attribute manlike or masculine qualities to her. The gender distinctions are blurry in their discourse. Âşık, in particular, adds more details to the gossip about her relationships, specifically with the so-called İskender. Âşık's successor, Kınalızâde Hasan Çelebi (1546–1604), pays more attention to the gossip than anything else. By the time Hasan Çelebi finished his *tezkire* in 1585/6, approximately seventy years had passed since Mihrî Hatun's lifetime. Yet his entry on her consists mostly of gossip, rather than information about her life and poetry. His work demonstrates how the *tezkire* genre became a tradition through recycling information from earlier examples. By Hasan Çelebi's time, anything written in *tezkires* had been established as fact, regardless of its veracity.

The significant outcome of such a process is that this discourse survives throughout the centuries and becomes the sole truth about women poets. For instance, from the seventeenth to nineteenth centuries, *tezkires* included no women writers at all. As I discussed earlier, this has little to do with the actual existence of women poets. Rather, it suggests another attitude change in literary history.[9] Throughout the classical period, Ottoman poetry became more refined. It became more strictly attached to its core values, making it more difficult for minor poets to find their way into the major histories. In the nineteenth century, however, we see a similar interest—as we saw in the sixteenth century—in women's marginalized inclusion in literary circles. As will be discussed in the last chapter of this book, the same discourse that was produced in the sixteenth century was used to present the women poets in the nineteenth century. By ignoring this specific discourse within its historical process, stories about women such as Mihrî Hatun are recycled and, eventually, become the truth.

Erotically Humorous Discourse

The portrayal of women poets in the sixteenth-century *tezkires*, specifically in those of Latîfî and Âşık, showcase the male poets' response to common (mis)conceptions of women.

9. For a brief overview of women writers in Ottoman literary history, see Havlioğlu 2010b.

While including their female colleagues, they reveal the major concerns of their time, both at the social and aesthetic levels. As they respond to the misconceptions about women in their erotically humorous language, they welcome the woman poet to the field while also appropriating them into the gender construction of the literary tradition. The historical process of the discourse demonstrates that eroticism and humor lightens the air and entertains the reader while legitimating the existence of the woman poet. The lack of clear gender boundaries in the *tezkire* writers' discourse reflects the larger aesthetic system of Ottoman poetry.

The supposed love affair between Mihrî Hatun and İskender Çelebi is a commonly told story in entries about Mihrî. It is clear in Latîfî's passage that the ornate language creates an erotic scene in which her body is compared to a bow and İskender's to an arrow. Though he concludes by saying that the relationship did not take place, the deliberate speculation attracts attention and makes the reader want to know more about her and İskender Çelebi. It appears that an İskender Çelebi did, in fact, live during Mihrî's lifetime; Latîfî gives us his father's name, Sinan Paşa. Âşık Çelebi also mentions an İskender Çelebi in this period in another entry for the poet Makâmî, a friend of Mihrî's who was also from Amasya. Âşık notes that Makâmî was an imam (Muslim community leader) during Şehzâde Ahmed's tenure and that he taught the Qur'an to the children of İbrahim Paşa and İskender Çelebi (Âşık Çelebi 2010, 826–27). Thus, it seems likely that there indeed was an İskender Çelebi who lived at that time. However, he was probably not a poet or an artist and was therefore not included in major literary histories.

After the sexually explicit scene quoted earlier, Latîfî apologizes, in a way, to Mihrî by giving her an opportunity to defend herself. According to him, when she was confronted by her poet friends in the court of Şehzâde Ahmed, she said the following couplet:

> The sweet water of my ruby lip sent many Alexanders
> In search of water and sent them back still thirsting[10]

Obviously, there are no historical grounds for this story and this couplet is not present in Mihrî's divan. Nevertheless, Latîfî's gossip lasted throughout the centuries to the present day. His first follower, Âşık Çelebi, also mentions this story, as did Kınalızâde, the third *tezkire* writer, who simply copied almost everything in Latîfî's entry for Mihrî (Kınalızâde Hasan Çelebi 1989, 934).

The İskender story and similar accusations question the morality of a woman who is involved in the field of poetry and is in contact with beloveds in the *meclis* culture. According to Âşık Çelebi, some men asked for Mihrî's hand—such as Paşa Çelebi, the Müderris of Eyüp Medresesi—yet she refused them all.

When Paşa Çelebi, the professor of *medrese* of Eyüp, asked for her hand, Zâtî composed the following lines:

> We heard that the Paşa has asked for Mihrî's hand
> Should she submit to him?
>
> This woman who has fasted for many years, poor thing
> Should she now make a feast with a donkey's cock? (Âşık Çelebi 2010, 832–36)

Mihrî did not mention Paşa Çelebi's name in her poetry. However, another poet, Zâtî, refers to this incident in a poem.

10. For Latîfî's *tezkire* I will rely on Andrews and Kalpaklı's (2005, 201) translations. There are many copies of this text and Andrews and Kalpaklı considered all of them in their translations.

His couplet is yet another example of an erotically humorous comment about her supposed affairs.

It is necessary to explore the meanings of Zâtî's poem to highlight its congruity with the erotically humorous discourse used to discuss women. In these two couplets, he conveys the strange and complicated matter of Paşa Çelebi's proposal. First, he introduces the supposed lack of sexual intercourse for a woman who has remained unmarried all her life. Zâtî communicates this through an analogy to the religious duties within Islam, and how those duties can be interrupted with feasts such as Ramadan. He uses words or phrases to remind the reader of this analogy, such as fasting (*oruç tutmak*) or breaking the fast (*oruç bozmak*). However, when he compares Paşa to a donkey, the imagery of religious duties and festivities are complicated by an erotic joke. He further indicates the strangeness of the incident by constructing a stark juxtaposition between the earthly and the heavenly, or the sensual and the spiritual, by inserting the grotesque image of the donkey's penis. The animal nature of earthly life, as opposed to spirituality, is so coarse that it provokes us to grasp the double meaning of the poem: the first and obvious meaning is that, for some reason, Paşa and Mihrî would make an odd couple; the second and contradictory meaning is that suppressing natural instincts might lead to abundant sensuality. By implication and through its ambiguity, the layers of meaning suggest the use of witticism (*nükte*), which highlights the value of the poem.

While the *tezkire* writers elaborate on the issue of love and lovers, they also try to protect Mihrî's reputation with the same erotically humorous discourse. In the following passage, we see Âşık Çelebi explicitly emphasizing her virginity and purity while he mixes and matches female and male characteristics:

> She made her love poems' virgins of meaning as her own with the dowry [*mehr*] of verse and brought them to her bridal chamber of [carnal] pleasure. In the lovely poems [where] she describes beautiful beloveds there is the virginal quality of Joseph. While the male poets had a craving for virgins of meaning, being a woman [herself they] came cheap. Although in her poetry there are some indecent words, that [kind of] menstrual fluid comes from the male gender, and they [women] see [morally] deficient expressions and, being of the class that needs guidance, are affected by this influence. (Andrews and Kalpaklı 2005, 203)

Âşık Çelebi introduces her as a modest, virginal, and pious woman on the one hand, and as a lover who chases beloveds on the other. The morally acceptable social roles for women in Âşık Çelebi's time were limited: a "virgin girl," a "married pious woman," or a "widow," all of who were defined by a male counterpart. However, he introduces another category for women, a moral promiscuous woman:

> Her writing is like a woman's embroidery, her composition is whorish. [As they say] a male lion is a lion but isn't a lioness a lion too, she was not free of beloved-chasing. (Âşık Çelebi 2010, 832–36)

The comparison of her virginity to that of Yusuf is also paradoxical in terms of gender associations. In the Qur'anic parable and subsequent legends, Yusuf was the paragon of both male beauty and chastity. Though virginity is not necessarily a required quality for men, Mihrî's supposed virginity is compared to that of a virtuous man. Âşık Çelebi's comparison between Mihrî and Yusuf may seem to be a contradiction, but it is permissible within the aesthetics of Ottoman literature. Curiously, in her poetry, Mihrî never represents herself as

Yusuf, but rather as Züleyhâ, a decision that will be discussed in detail in the following chapters.

Just as Âşık Çelebi measures her chastity by drawing a parallel between her purity and that of Yusuf, he compares her poetry to the menstrual fluid of men. In the Ottoman tradition, poetry requires the poet to use the discourse of love, use an erotic vocabulary, and be intimate with other poets—who happened to be almost always men—in court gatherings. Âşık says that Mihrî used "indecent words" in her poetry, which are attributed to men with the notion of male "menstrual fluid." Besides the gender conflict, male poets are like women who cannot avoid their nature during certain periods.

The complexities of including a woman in a male-dominated space such as poetry were striking and problematic and, for that reason, Âşık represents the situation as a conflict in the subject's gender. The subject of "menstrual fluid" is naturally expected to be about a woman and, similarly, "indecent words" are expected to belong to a man. However, the odd notion of a man's menstrual fluid parallels that of a woman saying indecent words, that is to say, writing poetry. By setting up this paradox in figurative language, Âşık explains the uniqueness of her situation. He continues his rhetoric about gender in the context of poetry by making a smooth connection between the phrase *bikr-i mana*, meaning "virginal meanings," and new concepts or imagery, and eventually to the virginity of Mihrî herself. The concept of imagination as the core of poetic language is compared to virginity, which happened to be a quality expected from women. A male poet looks for *bikr-i mana*, or unconquered territory, in his poetry, just as he looks for a virgin girl for marriage. It is a claim of masculinity that refers to ownership and honor.

Âşık praises Mihrî's talent in creating new meanings and says that doing so, as a woman, is not only natural for her, but also makes *bikr-i mana* easily attainable for her, while some inept male poets "crave" such talent. The words he uses for craving are *aş irmek*, a phrase that is used specifically in reference to pregnant women who crave odd things. Again, he plays with the notions of gender in language, describing a male situation with a phrase that refers to a female condition.

The allusive language suggests that, although she was in the business of writing love poetry, Mihrî was not an indecent woman and was a proficient enough poet. Âşık insists on representing Mihrî as a chaste virgin girl as well as a poet, though he does not feel the need to take such a stance with respect to a male poet. He does introduce male poets in terms of their moral values, but their virginity is never an issue.

No matter how well she composes poetry, to save her, she must be pronounced "chaste." Âşık concludes his argument in the following passage by explicitly stating that Mihrî came into this world a virgin and left as one:

> As it is with this woman-of-a-world, other than the glass of love no [stranger's] foot entered her sanctuary, no [miser's greedy hands] touched her [hidden treasure] and, other than ambergris and jewelry, hugged her neck. She came to this world a maiden and left it as a maiden. (Âşık Çelebi 2010, 832–36)

Âşık emphasizes that the love she wrote about was only a platonic love, as required in poetry. He presents some complicated comparisons in an attempt to explain her situation. First, he employs a common comparison of this world to a wretched woman from whom nobody can get what he or she wants. Then he compares that woman to Mihrî and claims that she, too, did not give anyone what they wanted from her. Other than the glass of love, nobody could succeed in reaching her. She used perfumes and jewelry, but nothing and no one else hugged her neck. He finishes with a strong statement of her everlasting virginity.

Like Âşık, Latîfî explains in the following section that, although she was beautiful and wrote poetry, this did not mean that she was not a respectable woman:

> They tell that, while she was so much a female beloved who worshipped beloved [men] and was so familiar with love and carnal passion, the hem of her modesty and the train of her chastity were clean of any stain of suspicion [*töhmet*] and she as a fearlessly pure person to whose shins the waves of the sea never reached. They go so far in [describing] her modesty and chastity [as to say] that she guarded the sanctuary of her presence from people outside her family and her hidden treasury from the [most poisonous] snake, that neither was the silvery nacre [of her oyster] swollen by droplets from the April [showers] of [sexual] union nor was her colorful [rose]bud watered by dew from the cloud of conjunction; in short, no one tasted of her two-part pomegranate, and no one cast a fish into her silver pool. (Andrews and Kalpaklı 2005, 197)

It is worth noting that, in Mihrî's poetry, "virginity" as a concept does not appear. Likewise, her poetry does not reflect any effort on her part to represent herself as a chaste woman. On the contrary, she uses images and conceits of love and wine gatherings as much as her male colleagues. She also never mentions her marital status in her poetry. Nevertheless, from the perspective of *tezkire* writers, her choice to remain unmarried seems to help her perform as a poet.

Remaining unmarried throughout her life allowed biographers to use her "virginity" as a quality to her advantage. Her relationship with other men, either professional or personal, would create suspicion about her honor, and *tezkire* writers seem to employ her "virginity" to support her position as a respectable woman. Although we do not know the reasons, Mihrî's choice to remain single all her life was an important commitment for her career. *Tezkire* writers' attention to her virginity proves that she may have made this choice consciously. Her singleness not only implies her virginity, but also works as a shield to protect her honor, which was in danger in the field of poetry.

From the mid-fifteenth to the late sixteenth century, the very few women poets we know of (e.g., the Ottoman Zeynep Hatun, the Mughal Zeb-un-Nisâ, and the Mamluk 'Ā'ishah al-Bā'ūnīyya) also chose to remain single while they were active poets. All *tezkire* writers agree that Zeynep stopped writing poetry once she married:

> Mihrî shied away from marriage and spent her life unmarried until she died. [However,] Zeynep married, lived under her husband's command and she quit poetry and prevented contact with men. (Âşık Çelebi 2010, 591)

The last phrase clearly suggests that, upon her marriage, Zeynep stopped composing poetry and no longer interacted with men. Zeynep's decision and Sehî's reporting suggest that, while unmarried, women could compose poetry and have contact with men. However, when in wedlock, they abstained from performing poetry, which not only implies contact with men but also gender ambiguity. Marriage enforces gender roles, particularly for women in this period. In other words, the congruence between poetry and gender fluidity points to a significant aspect of poetic circles. Either through the act of writing poetry or presenting it in a *meclis*, a woman had to free herself from social obligations, which could be difficult to do as a married woman.

Other than this reason, we do not know why Zeynep had to stop writing poetry or why Mihrî never married. Andrews and Kalpaklı (2005, 216) suggest that being a wife, which implied being sexually active, also required a woman to observe certain social restrictions. In addition to the social obligations a marriage would bring into their lives, wives represented their husbands' honor. These restrictions did not allow a woman to use the poetic language of love, which was considered indecent in society at large, though it was apparently accepted in private literary circles. I would add to the argument made by Andrews and Kalpaklı that a married woman promises her love to one man, whereas a poet has to practice love to many beloveds. This kind of loyalty is not expected from a man, as he could have up to four wives and many more concubines. A woman poet must be single to practice poetry, that is, to use the language of love and to express love for many beloveds.

Apart from the detailed discussions of her relationships with men and her morality, Mihrî's beauty was also commonly discussed. Âşık states that, though she was veiled, Mihrî's beauty was well known and that it was as exquisite as her poetry:

> According to the saying, "The woman is [all] a private part [that should be covered]," this chaste one was veiled but the beautiful voice of the bride of her natural talent arose from the horizon of her modesty and her poetry became as famous as her beauty. That gazelle hunted the valleys of rhetoric with the lasso of poems and the bow and arrow of the ambergris-scattering pen.
>
> **Couplet:**
>
> It is no shame for the sun to be feminine
> And no pride for the moon for of its masculinity. (Âşık Çelebi 2010, 832–36)

As expected from chaste women, Âşık informs us that Mihrî was veiled, but her voice rose beyond her veil and, through her voice, everyone knew of her beauty. Interestingly, Âşık is the only *tezkire* writer who felt compelled to mention her veil as a part of her visual appearance.

Latîfî also employs a paradoxical language in discussing Mihrî's poetry and makes interesting statements about femininity and masculinity:

> Although the coquettishness of her poems and the mannerisms of her speech are feminine, in burning and being consumed [by passion] she is like a [male] lover, and in the expression of passion and pleading [to be loved in return] she is masculine. (Andrews and Kalpaklı 2005, 198)

Latîfî makes a distinction between the masculine and the feminine based on ability to pursue a lover or skill of poetry. Although Mihrî's status as a woman interferes with what she does, because she performs poetry according to its rules, that is, in a manly manner (*merdane*), she is able to take part in the field. Both Sehî and Latîfî treat women poets differently, but for Sehî, women poets' biological gender is the reason to put them in a separate category, whereas for Latîfî it is not. Latîfî does not separate women poets into a different category; instead, he emphasizes Mihrî's gender either as masculine or feminine in terms of her poetic performance. Through the language he employs in his entry of Mihrî, he differentiates her gender as situational.

For Latîfî, the art of poetry, and the discourse of love that it necessitates, is a masculine job. From the perspective of poetry, which is the practice of high culture, a woman's presence in this field complicates the gender construction. Thus, Latîfî feels the need to explain that, although Mihrî is a woman, she is masculine enough to be a poet. Âşık follows this model and makes a similar statement:

> Although she is a woman, when there is no man in the field of men, she is two-women. (Âşık Çelebi 2010, 832–36)

Âşık presents Mihrî as a woman in the arena of poetry where male warriors fight. He states that, although she is a woman, she can fight twice as hard. In this respect, Mihrî traverses the border between the male and female worlds. Though she is a woman, Mihrî plays the game of poetry according to its rules. That is to say, she composes her poetry in the strict norms of court poetry, which were established for a male subject position. The word he uses for woman, *zen*, means not only "woman" but also "to kick, hit, or strike." Thus, the passage means that, although she is a woman, she is worth two women in the world of men, whereas some men are not worthy of being a man.

With this elaborate language, Âşık tries to explain that he judges Mihrî's poetry to be better than that of a deficient male poet, meaning a male poet who either cannot compose well within the rules of poetry or does not belong to the poetic community at all. He refers to the field of poetry as an arena of warriors, *merd-i meydan*. A woman's presence in a field of men can only be explained convincingly by the conclusion that she is exceptional for her gender but also a much better poet in comparison to deficient male poets. This is the reason that she can be accepted and included in this field.

The major characteristic of the *tezkire* writers' discourse is the gender conflict they tried to solve while talking about women. By highlighting the poet as a *merd*, or man, they highlight Mihrî's marginal position as a woman poet. After setting up this conflict, they continue with their elaboration on the gender of poetic expression. To solve this paradox, they purposefully mix and match gender assignments. This rhetoric suggests multiple relevant points. First, *tezkire* writers were aware of the gender of the poet, which was clearly a manly male. I explore this complicated issue in the next chapter when I evaluate Mihrî's statements of manliness or poethood. Second, a woman had to be extraordinary, or "exceptional" in Ann Rosalind Jones's (1986) terms, to be included in the gendered space of poetry. In Mihrî's case, her "virginity" is underscored not only as a shield against accusations about her professional and personal relationships with men, but also as value for her composition. The interesting connection between her "virginity" and the term *bikr-i mana* shows that *tezkire* writers presented her as the new actor in the poetic world. They explain her accepted existence in the world of poetry through her exceptional situation: her ever-virgin, gender-less status. Like her pen name, Mihrî's "virginity" is a part of her persona in the world of poetry.

After Latîfî and Âşık, Kınalızâde Hasan Çelebi (1989, 934) retells the story of Mihrî without making many changes. After Âşık, no *tezkire* writer expands on Mihrî's life story. Kınalızâde's entry is much shorter than that of Âşık or Latîfî. However, the gossip about Mihrî's relationships with men and her exceptional virginity are maintained in Kınalızâde's discourse. In his biographical sketch of Mihrî, he draws upon the work of Latîfî and Âşık, employing almost the same vocabulary, phrases, and anecdotes. His *tezkire* allows us to note how, as time passes, the objective information shrinks, but the narrative and commentary in *tezkires* either grow or remain the same.

2

Meclis as a Space of Artistic Production

I was hoping he would come with his tousled hair tonight
That I would make my soul a moth to his cheek's candle
tonight

Suddenly a host of ugly people entered and I said,
"Did Solomon loose his monsters on us tonight?"

A troop made for hanging gathered at the party
I wonder where to find a rope for them tonight

Some were bald, some blind, some halt and lame
Whom did revolving fate make our companions tonight?

Look what the heavens did to Mihrî on the longest of
nights
It was heedless, brought them in, made them our guests
tonight[1]

In these lines, Mihrî describes an evening party that she attends in hopes of meeting with the beloved. She is speaking of a *meclis* gathering where poets, musicians, and artists mingle, compete with each other, and find patrons. One of the characteristics of a *meclis* is that it is a semiprivate setting, exclusively held for the host and his or her guests. Sultans and

1. See appendix, poem no. 26.

2. A male patron with female courtiers in a *meclis* entertainment. Detail, Topkapı Palace Museum Library, B. 408, "Album of I. Ahmed" (seventeenth century), fol. 19a.

rulers hosted regular *meclises* at their palaces, where aspiring poets and artists would try to become regulars. In fact, when an influential patron would move to another city—such as when a crown price ascended to the throne, as in the case of Bayezid II—his entourage would move with him. In early modern Ottoman times, the *meclis* was the place where the arts were produced, shared, and confronted. It was also the venue for artists to build their reputation and networks.

As I discuss in detail later in this chapter, Mustafa Âlî's etiquette book enumerates the expectations of a *meclis*. At a basic level, it brought refined people together to enjoy one another's company, arts, good food, and drinks. These were gatherings that cherished eloquence and appropriate social conduct. Moreover, though, the *meclis* was meant to bring together people who would be compatible in various ways. As we see in the above lines, for instance, Mihrî complains about the guests of one party. To her surprise, some disgraceful people, who should not belong to the literary circles, show up and ruin it for her. We do not know why exactly they do not fit in, but she describes them in a sarcastic tone, comparing the scene to an attack by the monsters of Solomon. According to the Old Testament and the Qur'an, Solomon had the ability to communicate with animals and rule over the demons and jinns. His *div*, the giant creature, stole Solomon's magic ring that allowed him to speak to all creatures. The people Mihrî compares to the monsters of Solomon are so ugly and/or ignoble that they are not worthy of being the companions of poets such as herself. Presumably, she is not pointing only to physical hideousness, but also to a deeper incompatibility with her taste. She did not like these people for some reason. The poem could refer to either a specific night or a time period when these people took over a certain *meclis*. It could be that they belong to another circle or another network of artists.

Mihrî's *gazels* about certain dates and occasions, such as the one mentioned above, are interesting because traditionally, as a genre, the *gazel* was not expected to denote a specific time, date, or occasion. Only the poems that include hidden chronographs mention dates.[2] Occasions such as springtime, religious festivals, or even an evening conversation, are mentioned in *kasîdes*, which were written for public occasions. *Gazels*, on the other hand, were conceptualized as a type of abstract and idealized expression. Walter Andrews and Mehmet Kalpaklı

2. In these types of poems, each letter has a numeric value and when the numeric value of each letter in the verse is added up, the poem reveals a date.

(2005, 85) have responded to this common belief in Ottoman literary studies that *gazels* cannot be realistic. They suggested that "many gazels have double natures . . . they are produced both for idealistic, aesthetic purposes and for the most mundane of goals—to make a living, to attract a patron, to ask for a job, to write a letter, to celebrate an occasion, to seduce a beloved, to impress a friend." Likewise, *gazels* could serve as private entertainment for social functions because they were shorter and could be recited or sung to music. As Andrews and Kalpaklı (2005, 90) claim, by the sixteenth century, Ottoman love poetry had become a target for religious criticism for being too worldly. This attack was based on change in the poetic discourse as it evolved into a more realistic style. Specifically, the kind of love represented had moved from the spiritual to the profane.

Mihrî's occasional *gazels* are significant because they reflect a community and practice of entertainment, that is, they reflect the *meclis* culture in which she was involved as a poet. In this time period, poetry was not written to be read in private out of a book; it was meant to be recited in front of an audience. As Halil İnalcık (2010, 9) explains, in the Ottoman patrimonial system, as opposed to the printing press that allowed access to a larger audience, artists needed the protection and financial support of the ruler, the sultan. High culture in such a patrimonial state was centered around the palace. This does not mean that popular or folk literature was not present. Using the Medici family as an example, İnalcık purports that, before modernity, the situation in Europe was similar to that of the Ottoman Empire. Because of this kind of patronage system, we see urban centers emerge, such as Florence and Venice in Europe, Samarkand, Tabriz, Herat, Delhi, and Istanbul in the East (10–11). The great artists were associated with their cities and their patrons. Mehmed II and Bayezid II tried to bring the great Persian poet Jâmî from Herat. Apparently Jâmî was happy at the Timurid court and did not consider moving to the Ottoman court in Istanbul.

In this framework, consequently, poetry is performative and its meanings are primarily related to a specific moment of aesthetic conventions and social history. Looking at the poetry from its performative nature will enhance our understanding of a genre that has long been dismissed by modern Turkish literary studies for being too abstract or repetitive.

A woman poet presents an excellent opportunity to analyze the performative nature of poetry for reasons fundamentally related to her gender. The fact that gender is a social construct and can be seen in her language as a woman poet showcases the social conditions that define poetry. Therefore, Mihrî's specific choices, such as relating an occasion and implying a specific audience or her self-representation in this context, are the conditions in which she demonstrates the strategies she used to insert herself into the field as a woman. The starting point for reading Mihrî's work, then, should address her gender and how it is constructed in its spatial and aesthetic dimensions.

Most poets who had divans spent their lives in one or more *meclises*. There were many reasons for a poet to be part of a *meclis*. Apart from reputation building and social networking, the most important reason was to find a patron. A patron did not always have to be a sultan or a prince; anybody who had social, political, or economic power could be a patron for a poet. The role of the *meclis* in literary production was not only significant for poets, but also for their patrons, as they also built their reputation with the help of their entourage of artists. For the poets, their livelihood and legitimation in the field depended on this necessary exchange. Therefore, the *meclis* was a space where the poetic discourse was constructed.

The *meclis* in the Near Eastern world, as Samer Ali (2010, 13–14) argues, has its roots in ancient Greek practices that can be traced back to Plato's *Symposium*. With the Abbasid rule, however, it became the way not only to conduct administration, but also the production of knowledge and the arts. *Meclises* were "one of the many social institutions that promoted in varying degrees humanistic edification, which produced generations of professional and amateur humanists or littérateurs (adîb; pl. udabā)" (15). Medieval Islamic *meclises*, similar to later ones in Christian Europe, were places where students in various areas of study could acquire a liberal arts education. It is no coincidence that the major ancient Greek works were translated from Greek to Arabic and, in this way, survived thanks to Abbasid *meclises* of the ninth century.

In terms of artistic production and entertainment, the *meclis* had a significant place in classical Persian and Ottoman cultures. As Halil İnalcık (2011) points out, there were two significant aspects of a sultan's life: war (*razm*) and entertainment gatherings (*bazm*). What we know about the *meclis* as a physical space is limited to its depictions in works such as *işretnâmes* (the book of parties), *sakinâmes* (the book of the cupbearer), and the miniatures that accompany poetry in these works or that depict ceremonies at the palace. Like any other narrative poem, these works begin with prayers acknowledging the oneness of Allah (*tevhîd*, *münâcât*, and *naat*), register various *meclis* gatherings in detail, and finish with a repentance (*tövbe*), suggesting the poet's awareness of the worldliness of the drinking party. Based on the representations in these works, we can surmise that a *meclis* could be both inside, such as in a salon in the palace, a courtyard, a coffeehouse, a tavern, or a shop (the poet Zâtî's shop was a well-known gathering place for the poets in the sixteenth century), or outside, such as in a garden (İnalcık 2011, 192).

Regardless of its physical qualities, the *meclis* is a conceptual space that is constructed through social practices and, in return, the reiteration of social practices reproduces the space. The perpetual reproduction of space and its social practices maintain the tradition. By the end of the sixteenth century, as can be seen in the newly emerging etiquette books at the time, the Ottomans had established their own conventions for the *meclis* practice. In his book of etiquette, *Kavâʿidü'l-Mecâlis*, Mustafa Âlî lists the rules of *işret meclisi* (drinking parties.)[3] The participants were to be carefully selected and accepted through their manners, such as their behaviors and gestures. To be accepted into this circle, one had to perform the practices well enough to be a member. Âlî clearly suggests certain kinds of food and drink to be consumed at the gatherings, as well as certain behaviors to avoid insulting the host. There were appropriate activities for a sophisticated gathering, such as poetry reading, dancing, shadow theater, telling jokes, and playing chess. The invitees were expected not only to participate in such activities, but also to behave in an elegant manner. According to Âlî, a *meclis* could only be entertaining if the people invited were refined and the servers beautiful youths and women. He specifically describes the correct ways in which to perform poetry and respond to it. He even states that it would be rude to openly express criticism of a performed work.

The production and practices of the *meclis* are apparent in the narratives of the *tezkires*, but they can also be found within poetry. Arabic, Ottoman, or Persian poems, as Halil İnalcık (2010) explains, should be considered as part of a patronage system. Thus, *kasîdes*, or any genre for that matter, can be read

3. İnalcık (2011) summarizes the rules of the *meclis* as codified by Mustafa Âlî.

as a way to map networks of power. Take, for example, the difference between Bâkî and Fuzûlî, the two most celebrated Ottoman poets of the classical age. Bâkî was the lucky one, endowed with the blessings of the imperial court in Istanbul. Fuzûlî, on the other hand, had always been out of the loop because he was living in Baghdad. For this reason, Fuzûlî composed his *Şikayetnâme* (A Book of Appeal) to criticize the sultan's negligence. From the viewpoint of the rules of the *meclis*, Fuzûlî's distance from the court could have been one of the reasons for his estrangement.

As a space, the *meclis* was constructed to produce poetry and poets. The physical space builds the discourse of poetry, and in return poetry generates the *meclis* as a space. Like words, poetic traditions, rhetoric, and literary conventions are citational, because they have always been said before. As Derrida suggests, the performativity of words is their power, and their effect resides in their repetition over time. In this framework, to understand the meaning of poetry, or any words for that matter, we must consider its time, place, and audience, as well as its speaker. A Butlerian performativity of gender operates in the space and, over time, develops into a social convention through structured modes of action, such as gestures, clothes, and habits, but also words and rhetoric. Through repetition and reiteration, certain values of gender are established. However, the possibility of alternative performativities always exist and women poets demonstrate how this can occur. As Butler (1988, 520) suggests: "If the ground of gender identity is the stylized repetition of acts through time, and not a seemingly seamless identity, then the possibilities of gender transformation are to be found in the arbitrary relation between such acts, in the possibility of a different sort of repeating, in the breaking or subversive repetition of that style." While the *meclis* constructs the male poet as the speaker, it also points to the outsider, the woman poet, as the necessary other. Therefore, as she speaks from her marginal subject position, her words are transgressive and subversive. Though visual representations of *meclis* culture hint at both same-sex and mixed gatherings, according to Âlî, the women most likely to be accepted within the *meclis* were always concubines.[4] He suggests that notable women had no business being with the men and that they preferred to stay at home. Those spending time with men were not considered *hatun*, a title given to a woman whose status is equal to that of a man (İnalcık 2011, 184). Interestingly, Âlî simply ignores the existence of women poets who had the title, such as Mihrî Hatun.

Despite Âlî's comments on women, Islamic exegeses do not propose clear-cut boundaries between male and female spaces. As Irvin C. Schick (2010, 70) explains, "Contrary to received opinion, the relegation of Muslim women to the internal half of a bisected space is not clearly mandated by the Qur'an; indeed . . . not once does a derivative refer to women or women's quarters. Rather, this principle is based upon a particular reading of the so-called Verse of the Veil, which says, in part: 'And when you ask them [feminine] for something, ask from behind a hijab [veil/curtain]; that makes for greater purity for your hearts and for theirs.'" Though the debate over the identity of the feminine "them" used in this verse leans toward it being a reference to the Prophet's wives alone, veiling became an increasingly common practice after the Prophet's time. It allowed women to enter into male spaces, unlike men, who were not allowed into female quarters after puberty. Because of what is suggested in Islamic exegesis, we cannot expect to

4. Such depictions can be found in albums prepared for the sultan, such as Sultan Ahmed I's album (see Fetvacı 2012).

find a unanimous practice of gender segregation throughout Islamic history and in all areas where the religion is practiced.

Meclis culture confirmed the set of qualities and expectations for a poet, one of which was his or her acceptance by other participants. The legitimacy of a poet did not derive from a diploma or a literary school; it was confirmed by a group of people as a kind of communal acceptance. This aspect of poetry worked both as an advantage and a disadvantage for women. On the one hand, there was no need to attend an educational institution, such as a *medrese*, which would have been reserved exclusively for men. On the other, the female poet would have been forced to align herself with men to be accepted into the poetic world. In the premodern world, this could be very difficult for a woman because all participants were constructed to be male. Whereas for a male poet, his gender worked as a passport, for a female poet, her gender automatically cast her as an outsider. The spatial boundaries of the *meclis* were built through gender segregation. Constructing a group (women) as outsiders allowed the insiders (men) to exercise power over the women, as they are the ones that control the boundaries. The spatial borders of the *meclis* in terms of gender are not only physical, but also artificial. Because of the different experiences of men and women in the *meclis*, their artistic production should be treated accordingly.

Although there is no evidence of a women-only *meclis* occurring in Mihrî's lifetime, we may assume that it existed based on what we know about the later periods. From the late sixteenth century onward, there are strong suggestions of women's participation in *meclis* gatherings, as well as poetry devoted to women. Among the women patrons of the late sixteenth and seventeenth centuries, based on the poetry written for them, were Safiye Sultan, Mihrimâh Sultan, and the poet

Ayşe Hubbî Hatun.[5] In the nineteenth century, we have textual evidence of female gatherings hosted by female poets and patrons, such as Âdile Sultan, Moralızâde Leylâ Hanım, or Nigâr Binti Osman.[6]

The following poem by Mihrî suggests a gathering where women were present. Although she does not mention a specific name, she discusses a sick visit—most likely a visit to a royal person who happens to be sick. In the poetic world, it was uncommon to depict the beloved as a sick person. Therefore, it is possible that she is discussing a real-life situation in which she wrote the poem for a member of the royal family who was both sick and prepubescent at the time.

> At every moment, good health is fitting for you, the
>   blessed one
> At every instant, comfort is fitting for that pure body of
>   yours[7]

As the poem opens, she addresses a person who is depicted as blessed and pure. From the tone of these opening lines, it is clear that the sick person has status. Although this could simply be an anonymous beloved, the following lines build a sense of elevated status of the addressee:

> In a sublime dwelling, night and day, with joy and
>   pleasure
> Converse with a lovely woman in the health-fitting
>   courtyard

5. For poems written to honor women, see Havlioğlu and Aynur 2013.

6. For a further discussion of female *meclises* in later periods, see Havlioğlu 2010b.

7. See appendix, poem no. 34.

Mihrî praises him with reference to his home, depicted as a sublime residence. In the second couplet, Mihrî tells us more about what this person should do at home. She says that it befits him to have joy, pleasure, and conversation with lovely women. The image of this person with his exceptional residence and conversations with women likely indicates that she is discussing a harem, or the female quarters of his home.

> May pain be distant from that delicate body of yours,
> For your enemy torment in the house of grief is fitting

The royal person is apparently sick, and Mihrî hopes for such pain to leave him. As the imagery of sickness develops, she notes the issue of his enemies. It is not him, but his enemies who should be sick:

> Why does a fever grip you, let it grip your infidel rival
> For you good health, for your enemy, pain and
> degradation are fitting

Though it is he who has the fever, she wishes for his fever to be transferred to his infidel rival. Traditionally, the rival is the third person who interferes between the lover and the beloved. The rival is the poet's enemy, as he competes for the attention of the beloved. Here, Mihrî makes him the beloved's enemy as well:

> In order to cut off the head of your enemy with the sword
> of wrath
> For you boldness, and for your arm strength are fitting

While discussing his enemy, she introduces the scene of a warrior killing, or cutting the head off, the enemy with his sword of wrath. She depicts the warrior's personality as bold and his arms as strong, so he appears to be heroic. This couplet confirms that the sick person is important—someone who has significant status and the ability to fight like a warrior:

> May the one who envies you ever wail like the reed-flute
> For you, merrymaking with harp and dulcimer is fitting

She further elaborates in her poem, referencing a *meclis* gathering and its musical instruments. The *ney* (flute) is a traditional instrument whose sound is often compared to a lover's sigh. The sighs of sickness do not befit the role of the beloved. By setting up a *tezat* (opposition) between him and the envious ones, she wishes suffering upon the jealous ones, who should sigh like a *ney*, while the beloved enjoys life with other instruments.

> May God spare your life for your mother
> Whose one and only you are, for you, eminence is fitting

After all of the masculine imagery used to describe the sick person, such as his lordship or warrior-like qualities, in the seventh couplet, she suddenly depicts him as a son. Although he is powerful and important, he is still the son of a woman. This part of his personality, in which he is not superior anymore, is an interesting detail in this poem. He can be bold and courageous on the battlefield, but when he is sick, he is depicted as the dear son of his mother. He is her only son and for that reason eminence befits him. In this sense, he could be anybody, but he would still be the most important person to his mother. This couplet is very unusual, as Mihrî brings this divine lord's mother into the picture, showing his soft side. Besides the fact that this is a personal choice likely based on her perspective as a woman—as she brings another woman into the discussion—it also disrupts the abstract image of the powerful beloved, and it represents him as a human being.

> Praise God, Mihrî, your well-wisher could visit you
> Those who see you say "to you (such) pillars of prosperity
> are fitting"

In the final signature couplet, she adds one more related phrase to her depiction: *erkân-ı devlet* (pillars of prosperity), confirming that the important person that the poem was written for was most likely her patron, Şehzâde Ahmed. Through reading the clues in this poem, we can envision a scene in which Ahmed is sick and Mihrî writes a poem to wish him health, performing it during her sick visit. We can imagine this taking place in the harem with Şehzâde Ahmed's mother also present, as Mihrî mentions women indirectly, in the background. She implicitly addresses the mother, acknowledging her, as she must have been very sad at her son's illness.

Mihrî's use of space to construct her gendered identity is legitimate as she remains in the confines of poetic tradition. First, the poem is a product of a *meclis* gathering, and second, it utilizes stock imagery to depict the beloved and his surroundings. However, she makes subtle interventions, such as the sudden change of perspective in terms of depicting the beloved as a son. Likewise, her inclusion of the mother in the picture suggests a female gathering. Both of these points can be evaluated as a woman's stylistic choices.

In the later chapters of this book, I define a pattern of composition developed by Mihrî. Through considering the performative nature of poetry and of being a poet, as shown in this poem, the gender of the poet offers an opportunity to adopt alternative approaches to reading poetry. For this kind of reading, a woman poet can be instrumental, as her work views tradition from the outside and her existence and words challenge the tradition and disrupt it from within. Her lines force us to consider the space in which they were produced and how they functioned. They also represent a shift in the aesthetic discourse, as she depicts a nontraditional beloved with his weaknesses. In the next chapter, I continue to focus on the performativity of poetry, particularly its discourse of love, and I situate Mihrî's poetry within this discursive tradition.

3

City and Patron as Beloveds

Amasya and Bayezid II

Alas, Mihrî, your life has passed in Amasya
If you are wise, do not go back, stay in Constantinople.[1]

Mihrî was born in the vibrant city of Amasya, one of the significant urban centers during her lifetime. Her hometown, the space of her family, education, and networking, seems to be the most important factor in her becoming a poet. The city of Amasya was a place especially useful for poets and intellectuals to form networks and alliances among notable people who were potential patrons. As the eastern frontier of the empire, it was the administrative and cultural center of Eastern Anatolia and the place where most crown princes served as governors, for which reason it was known as the *şehzâdeler şehri*, the city of crown princes. This meant not only continuous monetary support, but also a substantial amount of endowed pious funds, most of which came from prominent families and the sovereign family. During Mihrî's lifetime, there were nine mosques, ten *medreses*, four convents, six public kitchens, fifteen hammams, and one *dârüşşifâ* (hospital) in Amasya.[2]

1. See appendix, poem no. 4.

2. This hospital was founded by the Seljuks in 1309. Sabuncuoğlu Şerefeddin, one of the major doctors who served there for approximately

3. A depiction of Amasya. Bozoklu Osman Şakir, "Musavver İran Seyahatnâmesi," 1810. The Directorship of the Manuscripts of Turkey, Millet Manuscript Library 822, fol. 52.

When *şehzâdes* ascended to the throne, they usually paid dues to the city where they had served as governors, as they considered this city to have given them the support they needed to become sultan. For instance, after his enthronement in 1486, Bayezid returned the favor to Amasya by building glorious monuments, such as the Bayezid complex, which had a mosque, a *medrese*, a primary school, and a public kitchen.[3] Being the crown prince of a significant urban center was

fourteen years, wrote his *Cerrâhiyye-i İlhâniyye* in Turkish, in which he explained operations with drawings (DIA, "Bîmâristan," vol. 6, 163–78.

3. DIA, "Beyazıd II Camii ve Külliyesi," vol. 6, 40–49.

considered a first step toward the throne. A powerful city was so influential that it could make a sultan.

There were many names for this city, accentuating its geopolitical and artistic importance: Bağdâdü'r-Rûm (Baghdad of Anatolia), Medînetü'l-Hükemâ (the city of philosophers), or Medreseler Şehri (the city of colleges). From 1421 onward, the Ottomans ruled the city. Its glory days were throughout the end of the fifteenth and beginning of the sixteenth centuries, particularly during Bayezid II's rule.

Investment in the city was also a way of constructing power for women in the sociopolitical context. Ülkü Bates (1978, 245) has suggested that, during the Seljuk and early modern Ottoman periods, women participated in public and political life through sponsoring important buildings, such as mosques, fountains, and schools. Amasya is a good example of Bates's assertion. Gülbahar Hatun (one of Bayezid's favorites and Ahmed's mother) and Bülbül Hatun (Ahmed's favorite) had endowment funds in the city. It was quite common for mothers of *şehzâdes* or sultans to establish endowment funds to make themselves more important and visible to the public—a precaution for future unfortunate events. As Hasan Karataş (2011, 52) suggests, Gülbahar Hatun's concern for her family is visible in her strategy of securing her properties by endowing certain villages and the Enderun Mosque. Had she known that Bayezid would be sultan, she would not have needed to be so cautious. But, as in Bülbül Hatun's case, they are not always lucky: Ahmed was unable to succeed his father to the throne. When Bülbụl's son Ahmed was struggling for the throne, she followed in Gülbahar's footsteps and endowed the same mosque. However, as Karataş notes, Bülbül Hatun designated her daughters as the legal benefactors of her endowment. Karataş interprets Bülbül Hatun's decision as a "precautionary measure" to protect the female members of the family.

Another example of women creating voices in Amasya through architecture is still visible today. In the Hatuniye district of present-day Amasya, one may still find the Hatuniye Mosque, which also houses a *sıbyan mektebi* and a public kitchen.[4] This complex was commissioned by Bülbül Hatun. Rather than establishing yet another public building accessible only to men, Bülbül Hatun chose to sponsor a mosque with a primary school for boys and girls, a kitchen, and a hammam, which would serve all. Although we do not have documented evidence of women's social life during Mihrî's time, we can speculate, based on Gülbahar and Bülbül Hatun's architectural patronage, that the city had prominent women.

Mihrî's poetry reflects her sense of belonging to the city. Indeed, Amasya seems to have been an important factor in the lives of women poets. All three known women poets of the early modern era, Zeynep, Mihrî, and Ayşe Hubbî Hatun, came from Amasya. Nisâyî, Mehmet Çavuşoğlu's discovery, was also from Amasya. Although Istanbul was the new capital, poets showed a sense of affinity for their respective cities, such as Latîfî's affection for his hometown, Kastamonu. He was so biased in favor of his hometown that he falsely reported that some poets were from Kastamonu, including Zeynep (Latîfî 2000, 178).

Mihrî would not have succeeded without the support of the literary community of Amasya, which apparently allowed women poets to participate in the literary practice, unlike Istanbul or any other city at the time. She was clearly aware of the power of her city. Some of her poems were dedicated to Amasya, asserting her belonging to the city and making it one of her major beloveds. Consequently, the city of Amasya, with

4. DIA, "Hatuniye Camii," vol. 6, 500–501.

all its beauties, not only appears as an inspiration but also as an important ally in Mihrî's poetry. Her poems about Amasya encompass a sense of space and a reflection of the time during which she lived there. These poems give an accurate picture of the Amasya region, including the climate, flora, architecture, and important people of her time. For instance, in the following stanza from a poem written for the town of Lâdik in the Amasya region, there are direct references to geographical details:

> Its weather temperate, its waters like Kevser
> Its trees are pomegranate, cypress, and juniper
> Its herbage basil and hyacinth, its earth ambergris
> What a pleasant highland is this Lâdik town[5]

Lâdik is an ancient town in the countryside. It used to be within the borders of the Amasya region and was used during Şehzâde Ahmed's time as a summer residence. Its weather is indeed mild and the mountainous land is lush with all kinds of trees thanks to the Iris River (Yeşilırmak). As the poem progresses, Mihrî provides a list of flowers that grow in the city. After the geographical and botanical survey, she mentions the most important person in the city, Şehzâde Ahmed, and his summer palace, which is located at the top of a hill in Lâdik:

> A high-arched throne is constructed there
> Green leaves became an awning for it
> Within is that Monarch of the age
> What a pleasant highland is this Lâdik town

In most of her poetry about Amasya, Mihrî makes a connection between the city and its ruler. When she was younger,

5. For the full original poem, see Mihrî Hatun 2007, 327–31 (translation my own).

the ruler was Bayezid, but Bayezid's son Ahmed succeeded him and Mihrî wrote many poems for Ahmed. The following couplet is extracted from a poem comparing Şehzâde Ahmed's court to a hospital where the sick are cured:

> Because your court has become a hospital for those who
> ail,
> From you, to all who suffer, has come the cure of
> generosity[6]

Şehzâde Ahmed's court has a double meaning here: first, the actual building of the provincial palace, and second, his governorship. Mihrî adds one more meaning by comparing his court to a hospital for the sick. In the tradition of love poetry, lovers are depicted as sick and troubled due to the torments of love for the beloved. For that reason, they are usually pale and poor. Thus, the city of Amasya is full of lovers who are seeking a cure. In other words, this town is full of people who are very sensitive to emotional attachments, and who are therefore inclined to be excellent poets.

In reality as well as in poetry, Amasya was a vibrant province and many prominent poets lived there during Mihrî's time. The ultimate beloved in the city, that is, the most powerful person and patron of the lovers, was the *şehzâde*. He is the only one who could cure the lovers' illness. In this way, Mihrî's poem implies that the prince should take care of the poet-lovers of the city by giving them many awards. Furthermore, through an allusion to the *Dârüşşifâ* (asylum), constructed in Amasya between the years of 1308 and 1309, Mihrî makes a connection between the sickness of the lovers and the sickness of those seeking treatment in Amasya.

6. See appendix, poem no. 2.

Some of her poems for Amasya and its rulers are so affectionate that one might think she would never consider another patron or a court. This is logical, considering that the lifestyle of an Ottoman poet and his/her livelihood depended on patrons. In this framework, her relative affection for Amasya can also be read as a sign of her limited opportunities as a provincial poet who spent most of her life in the city.

Mihrî as the Woman Poet of Amasya

Mihrî's career as a poet was crucially related to the city and the influence of her family in the city. Mihrî came from an intellectual and spiritual family. Mihrî's grandfather, Pîr İlyas Şücaeddin Halvetî (d. 1410), was from Gümüşlüoğulları (Mehmed Zihnî 1877) and was the descendant of Baba İlyas,[7] the founder of the Amasya branch of the Halveti order. As Hasan Karataş (2011) discusses, the Halvetis were one of the major Sufi orders in Anatolia during the early modern Ottoman period and were particularly influential in the fifteenth and sixteenth centuries.

Mihrî's grandfather, Pîr İlyas Şücaeddin Halvetî, was a respected *şeyh* (religious/spiritual authority) of his time. Although Halvetis are not matriarchal (no Sufi orders in Anatolia were), women played significant roles in the organization and function of the convents. The tradition of women's participation was institutionalized occasionally as branches of the primary order, as in the case of Bâcıyân-ı Rûm (Sisters of Rome),[8] during the formational years of the Ottoman

7. The Babais played an important role in the emergence of the empire. They were widespread from southeast Anatolia to the Black Sea. The revolt happened in 1240 and the rebels were defeated by the Seljuk army.

8. Rum or Rome meant Anatolia at this time.

Empire.[9] Likewise, Alevi and Bektaşi women poets had always existed in Anatolia but, because their poems were often performed and transmitted orally, they have been overlooked by Ottoman literary studies.

Mihrî's father, Belâyî, was Hasan Çelebi ibn Yahya, a *kadı* of Amasya. We know little about Belâyî but, thanks to his daughter's poetry and fame, he is also mentioned in the *tezkires*, such as in the following passage from Latîfî (2000, 510):

> She was the daughter of a judge who wrote poetry under the penname of Belâyî from Amasya.

Mihrî also mentions her father's pen name in her own poetry:

> Oh Mihrî, having suffered many troubles, it is clear you
> are of the lineage of Belâyî [the Afflicted][10]

Likewise, Bayezid II's gift registry refers to Mihrî's full name, including her father's title and name: "The daughter of Mevlânâ Hasan from Amasya" (Erünsal 1981, 310).

Mihrî's success in poetry hints at her access, through her family, to education and prominent social circles. Her family history and her significance as a member of this family are still visible in Amasya today. Her family shrine in the Sofular district of Amasya consists of four family tombs, one of which is believed to be that of Mihrî Hatun (Hüsameddin 1986).

In early modern times, belonging to a prominent family was a ticket to education for both men and women. Although we have very limited information about Mihrî's life, we can make an educated guess that she was trained both at home and around the notable members of her family. The kind of

9. For a discussion of Bâcıyân-ı Rûm, see Kafadar 1993.
10. See Mihrî Hatun 2007, 235 (translation my own).

education needed to become a poet could not be acquired in an institution; it was done, instead, through traditional training. The relationship between master and apprentice was the way in which the arts were taught. Therefore, the question becomes not *if* she was educated, but *how* she was educated.

During Mihrî's time, *sıbyan mektepleri* (primary schools) financed by private individuals were available for boys and girls (Faroqhi 2000, 186). Although we do not know their exact numbers in Amasya, there were 134 *sıbyan mektebi* in Bursa, another important province (Hızlı 2001, 110). The numbers suggest that it was common to send children to these primary schools. As is clear from their curriculum, the main purpose of these schools was to teach students the basic practices of Islam. Apart from reading the Qur'an, they learned Islamic tradition, grammar, and moral ethics.

Only Evliyâ Çelebi (1614–72) suggests Mihrî Hatun's superior religious education and competence in his *Seyahatnâme*:

> She has a divan and poetry and writing on Islamic law, menstruation and puerpera. (Evliyâ Çelebi 2003, 142)

Although Evliyâ notes that Mihrî's religious poetry specifically focused on women's issues, I have not come across any poems on these themes in the available documents. However, it is possible that those poems—if they indeed existed—were not included in *tezkires* or her divan.[11]

Considering her heterodox family, it is also likely that she received education in Halveti Sufi convents. Schimmel (1975) notes that, especially within Sufi orders, women were allowed

11. Divans were not necessarily compiled by the poet. It was more common for a *müstensih* (copier) to do the job. Depending on its popularity, a divan could have many copies compiled by different copiers.

to give opinions on issues related to women.[12] Likewise, Dror Ze'evi (2006, 84) suggests that repeated references to women and regulation of sexes in Sufi gatherings implies women's existence in Sufi social practices. As her family founded the Halveti order, it is more than possible that Mihrî was brought up within the values of the convent.

Regarding Mihrî's relationship with Müeyyedzâde Abdurrahman Çelebi, Âşık Çelebi says she studied the subject of love with him by using the compound verb *mülâzemet etmek*:

> When Müeyyedzâde . . . was young and resident of Amasya, he first became acquainted with her and then acquired a glow by virtue of love. There was affection on her part [too], and later when Müeyyedzâde had taken the penname Hâtemî and became chief military magistrade [*kadıasker*] Mihrî for a time persisted [in her affection]. The late [Müeyyedzâde] made reference to the affair with innuendos and allusions [so] Mihrî composed this couplet and sent to him:
>
> > O Hâtemî, you lied Mihrî when you played the lover
> > By God, she loves you better than any boy (Âşık Çelebi 2010, 832–36)

According to George Makdisi (2012, 283), *mülâzemet* comes from the Arabic root word *lazama*, meaning "to be needed or required." *Mülâzim* is derived from the same root, meaning "studying fellow." The Turkish version of the same word, *mülâzemet etmek*, means "to study side by side with a master." In other words, it refers to the traditional manner of

12. As described by Annemarie Schimmel (1975) and Leila Ahmed (1992), mystical Islam allowed women to participate in gatherings and benefit from dervishes' teaching, as well as to become prominent mystical figures.

teaching by a master to his/her apprentice. It can also mean "internship."[13] Cem Behar (2012) explains the tradition of *meşk*, or practice, in terms of studying music in Ottoman times, but this kind of training was prevalent across the Ottoman lands in different periods. Complete submission to the master and the art form was reflected with an intimate learning style over a long period of time and numerous practice sessions.

Considering the *tezkire* writers' tendency toward speculation, it could be that Mihrî and Müeyyedzâde only had a professional relationship, but Âşık elaborates on different meanings in the poem. From Mihrî's lines in poem 9 in this book's appendix, it can be deduced that Müeyyedzâde wrote poetry for her (there is no record of it) and that she responds in this dialogue. The poetic tradition in which they speak to each other considers "love" a subject matter to study and "boys" inspirational beloveds. Even when the beloved was a woman, she would be depicted within the same poetic discourse. If we assume that Müeyyedzâde wrote a poem for Mihrî without mentioning her name, it is possible that it appeared as if he had written it for a boy. She corrects him, stating that she loves him more than a boy. Her statement maintains the ambiguity between two meanings: first, she says she loves him more than she loves any of these idealized boys of poetry, and second, she loves him more than any of these imaginary beloveds will ever love him. Either way, she claims to be a better beloved than any abstract or actual boys. The love of a boy is a traditional aesthetic or mystic/platonic love in poetry, but she challenges this tradition when she claims to be a better beloved than a boy. She presents herself as an alternative beloved to the mythic/platonic beloved boy and invokes the love relationship between

13. DIA, "Mülâzamet," vol. 31, 537–39.

4. A representation of Sultan Bayezid II. Topkapı Palace Museum Library, H. 1563, "Bayezid II" in Seyyid Lokmân Çelebi's *Kıyâfetü'l-insâniyye fi Şemâili'l-Osmâniyye*, fol. 50b.

a man and a woman. Although she most likely meant to refer to a professional relationship, any kind of love between a man and a woman was considered carnal desire and, for that reason, though studying love in this context meant studying poetry, it does not rule out the possibility of a romantic relationship.

Then again, all of Mihrî's professional relationships, particularly those with influential men, generated scrutiny.

Like any other poet, Mihrî's professional relationships with her colleagues were integral to her development and acceptance as a poet. Some of these relationships are apparent in her poems. Many of the poets she mentions were friends from the court of Şehzâde Ahmed, such as Güvâhî, Makâmî, or Necâtî, who also spent some time in Amasya.[14]

Bayezid II as the Patron

> Who is the Great Ruler, that is to say, Sultan Bayezid
> Until the resurrection, may his days on the face of the
> earth be countless[15]

Amasya was the site of origin for Mihrî as a poet because it provided the necessary components of her career. Her patron, Bayezid II, was also a significant factor. Bayezid's tenure as the governor of Amasya lasted from 1454 to 1481. He was just seven years old when he was appointed to Amasya as the prince-governor, along with his mother, Gülbahar Hatun, and his *lalas* (mentors) Ali Paşa, Çandarlızâde İbrahim Paşa, and Fenârizâde Ahmet Paşa (Kappert 1976, 19, 22, 45).[16] His father, Mehmed II, was insistent on his son Bayezid's thorough education. Growing up in Amasya, Bayezid had many teachers, such as Selâhaddin, who studied Mevlânâ al-Haravî's commentary on *Hidâyat al-Hikma* and Nasafî's *ʿAqâʾid* with him.

14. Mehmet Çavuşoğlu (1971, 18) chronicles Necâtî's life story and notes that he was either from Amasya or that he spent some time there.

15. Mihrî Hatun 2007, 189 (translation my own).

16. Kappert (1976, 22) suggests that this Ali Paşa should be Hızır Bey, who was sent to Turkmenistan by Murad II to bring a wife for his son Mehmed II.

His teachers taught him the Islamic and rational sciences, as well languages like Arabic, Persian, and a bit of Italian (Kazan 2010, 84). For instance, one of the leading mathematicians and astronomers of the time, Molla Mahmud b. Mehmed b. Kadızâde-yi Rûm, was among his teachers. The prominent calligrapher, Şeyh Hamdullah, also lived in Amasya and taught Bayezid and his friends, Müeyyedzâde and Tâcîzâde Câfer Çelebi (Müstakimzade Süleyman Sadeddin Efendi 1928, 185). Apart from his interest in calligraphy, he was an avid archer.

Although Müeyyedzâde (1456–1516) was nine years younger than Bayezid, he could enter the *şehzâde* palace because he came from one of the most prominent families of the city (Gibb 1900–1909, 2: 29). Müeyyedzâde was brought up within his family's heterodox Muslim heritage, which was originally from Iran (Kurnaz 1999).[17] His father was the *nişancı* (inscriber of the imperial monogram) of Bayezid II when the latter held his princely court in Amasya. Consequently, Müeyyedzâde became the *musâhib* (boon-companion) of Bayezid at a very early age.

When Bayezid's father, Mehmed II, heard rumors that Müeyyedzâde was a bad influence on Bayezid, he sent a decree for Müeyyedzâde's execution in 1479 (Gibb 1900–1909, 2: 29). According to rumors, Bayezid was addicted to alcohol and abused substances, and he spent his days with the poets and artists of the town. Bayezid immediately wrote back to his father asking for his forgiveness and explained that he was using those substances to prevent weight gain. Meanwhile, he arranged for Müeyyedzâde's exile. Müeyyedzâde shaved

17. Cemal Kurnaz (1999) explains that, from the time of Mehmed II onward, it is possible to trace the lines of migration from Iran to the territories of the Ottoman Empire.

his beard and immediately fled, disguised as a *derviş* (an ascetic). At the time of this incident, Bayezid was thirty-two and Müeyyedzâde twenty-three years old (Kurnaz 1999, 650). Müeyyedzâde went to Aleppo and then Shiraz to study with Jalâl-ad-dîn al-Dawânî. He spent four years in exile.

Although Âşık Çelebi (2010, 658) explains the incident as an innocent-seeming crime on Müeyyedzâde's part, Mehmed II was not happy about his son's Halveti friends. Bayezid had very strong ties within the Amasya community, most of whom were Halvetis, and Müeyyedzâde was among them. It would not be surprising if, with his harsh order to execute Müeyyedzâde, Mehmed II was looking for an excuse to threaten the Halveti community. Müeyyedzâde returned shortly after Bayezid's succession in 1483. He lived in Amasya for a short time before joining his friend in Istanbul. The first of his many administrative positions was that of *müderris* (professor at a higher-education institution) for the *medrese* of Kalenderhâne. Later, he served as *Anadolu kazaskeri* (military judge) of Anatolia, then as *Rumeli kazaskeri*. After Bayezid's death, he established a good relationship with Bayezid's son, Selim I, who ascended to the throne in 1512. Until his death in 1516, Müeyyedzâde supported many scholars and poets, such as Necâtî, Z*â*tî, Kemalpaşazâde, and Hâfız-ı Acem.

In light of this information about Müeyyedzâde and Bayezid, we can assume that Mihrî was friends with them when they all lived in Amasya until 1479. After that, Müeyyedzâde left Amasya and returned only for a month and a half. If we estimate that Mihrî was the same age as Müeyyedzâde, she must have been born around 1456.

After Bayezid's enthronement, Mihrî was not among the entourage that left with him and settled in Istanbul. She remained in her city Amasya and frequented Bayezid's son, Ahmed. However, at some point in her life, she presented her

TABLE I

Distribution of the Rewards Mihrî Received

Money (Akçe)	*Reason*	*Date*
3,000	Presented divan	914/1508
500	Unknown	914/1508
3,000	Unknown	915/1509
3,000	Presented *kasîde*	916/1511
1,000	Presented *kasîde*	917/1512

Note: Information in tables 1 and 2 is collected from Hilal Kazan's study of Bayezid II's gift registry. See Kazan 2010, 317, 332–33.

divan to Bayezid when he was sultan. Although we do not know exactly when she finished her divan, one of the remaining copies has the seal (*tuğra mührü*) of Bayezid II.[18] This means that, most likely, it was presented to him. Table 1 showcases the monetary awards Mihrî received from Bayezid II, based on his gift registry (*in'âmat defteri*). Table 2 shows the total amount of rewards she received in comparison to her contemporary colleagues, Zâtî, Makâmî, and Necâtî.

Based on these tables, we can assume that Mihrî was awarded around the same amount as Makâmî, but less than Zâtî and Necâtî. She did not receive any other form of rewards, though it was a common practice to present valuable clothing to artists.

Bayezid's gift registry might suggest that she was living in Istanbul for a while because, when Bayezid became sultan, his entourage (e.g., Müeyyedzâde, Tâcîzâde, and Şeyh Hamdullah) moved to Istanbul with him. However, there are no clear references in *tezkires* or other secondary sources that

18. Mihrî Hâtun Dîvanı, 3974 Ayasofya, Süleymaniye Libray, Istanbul.

TABLE 2

Rewards Mihrî Received in Comparison to Makâmî, Zâtî, and Necâtî

Name of Poet	*Total Money (Akçe)*	*Total Clothing*	*Date*
Mihrî Hatun	10,500 (over 5 instances)	Unknown	914–17/1508–12
Makâmî	10,400 (over 11 instances)	1 embroidered clothing	936–40/1530–34
Zâtî	14,000 (over 17 instances)	1 wickerwork, 1 felt clothing, 1 embroidered clothing	911–40/1506–34
Necâtî	13,000 (over 15 instances)	3 embroidered clothing	914–40/1508–34

indicate whether she went to Istanbul. Among later sources, Mehmed Zihnî's (1877) *Meşâhirü'n-Nisâ* states that Mihrî was among the Istanbul poets. Furthermore, Âşık's mention of the *müderris* of Eyüp, Paşa Çelebi, who asked for Mihrî's hand, is an interesting detail, as Eyüp is a district in Istanbul, not in Amasya. This may mean that Paşa Çelebi had met her in Istanbul and wanted to marry her. In addition to all these speculations, one of her poems compares Amasya to Istanbul:

Alas, Mihrî, your life has passed in Amasya
If you are wise, do not go back, stay in Constantinople[19]

19. See appendix, poem no. 4. Mehmet Arslan discusses reading the city's names as Konstantin, Konstantini, or Konstantiniyye and suggests that, although this line can be read as "If you are smart, stay in Istanbul," it is also possible to read it as "If you are smart do not go to Istanbul." He further suggests that, because the secondary sources (other than Mehmed

The following poem gives further credence to the assumption that Mihrî spent some time in Istanbul by suggesting a river or sea voyage on which Mihrî leaves her hometown and travels to somewhere else. Wherever she is going, she does not seem to be agonizing over leaving home. On the contrary, the poem has a sense of carpe diem and expresses the excitement she feels for new opportunities:

> Let's cast grief into the sea and be merry on board this ship
> Because this world does not endure, let's enjoy this
> moment.
>
> Mihrî, even though the heavens have put you far from
> your homeland
> The condition of exile is pleasant to many hearts
>
> Don't grieve for your wounded heart for once, a time will
> come
> When you will find a balm for it in the land of exile[20]

The poem opens, in the first couplet, with the scene of traveling on a boat. Mihrî commands herself to cast her grief to the sea and be happy while on the ship. She hopes for remedy in exile, for which she uses the word *gurbet.* This word specifically means being displaced and far from home. It is possible that she traveled to Istanbul and enjoyed the blessings of the big city. She might have gone to meet her friends there. In the previous poem, Mihrî clearly states that she spent most of her life in Amasya, so, if she did move to Istanbul,

---

Zihnî's *Meşâhirü'n-Nisâ*) do not mention her going to Istanbul, she probably did not go to Istanbul. However, *tezkires* do not say that she *did not* go Istanbul. It is simply not mentioned.

20. See appendix, poem no. 5.

it must have been later in her life. We do not know where she died, although the modern historian Hüseyin Hüsameddin claims that she is buried next to her grandfather, Pîr İlyas Halvetî, in the Sofular district of Amasya.[21] This tomb bears an inscription that states that Pîr İlyas is buried there along with his son-in-law, Pîr Celâleddin Abdurrahman Çelebi, his grandson, Pîr Hayreddin Hızır Çelebi, his wives, and four of his daughters (Hüsameddin 1986, 188–89). Mihrî's father's name is Hasan Çelebi, and since neither her father's name nor her own is mentioned in the inscription, it is not clear that she was buried there.

As I have attempted to show in this chapter, for *tezkire* writers, welcoming a woman poet to the male-dominated intellectual circles required some gender bending in the social and aesthetic space. Entries on Mihrî in *tezkires*, therefore, are an example of the gender construction of the Ottoman intellectual discourse of the sixteenth century, rather than her biography. By analyzing these documents in this light, their rather peculiar use of gender makes more sense. Mixing and matching the traditional binaries, such as men and women, with a dose of eroticism and humor is not only entertaining, but also fits well with the overall gender ambiguity of the Ottoman aesthetic discourse. *Tezkire* writers' narratives respond to the first major question developed in the previous chapter: what did it mean to be a woman in early modern Ottoman intellectual circles? *Tezkire* writers demonstrate that poetry was a male-dominated

21. Hüsameddin relates this information based on Evliyâ Çelebi's following assertion: "Ecdâd-ı 'izâmı Hazret-i Pîr İlyâs Asitânesinde defn olundı." Although I include information from Hüsameddin, I am not convinced with his arguments. As İsmail Erünsal suggests, Hüsameddin's suggestions are not based on evidence and are therefore not convincing. See Erünsal 1983 and Hüsameddin 1986, 99.

space and women were essentially marginal. To be included, women had to be appropriated. In other words, *tezkire* writers' discourse lays the groundwork for understanding the concepts of gender in Mihrî's time. Although "woman" represented temporality and temptation in this tradition, the *tezkire* writers' attempts to overcome this obstacle and welcome her in their world reveals the performativity of gender. For instance, the concept of "virginity" is both a confirmation of her morality as well as the appropriation of her gender or genderlessness as the new actor in the battlefield of poetry.

What *tezkire* writers do not address—although we may be able to read between the lines—are the realities of Mihrî's life and her socioeconomic background. Considering the *meclis* culture and patronage system of the intellectual circles through secondary sources alongside evidence from her own poetry demonstrates the main advantages of Mihrî's life story: she happened to be born in the right place and at the right time to become a celebrated woman poet. She was indeed the "lucky star" of her time, blessed with the fortunes of a privileged family, a vibrant city, and a generous patron.

We do not know if there were more women intellectuals other than Mihrî and her three contemporaries because the major histories do not mention them. The fact that Mihrî, Zeynep, Ayşe Hubbî, and Nisâyî could exist shows that there could be other women poets whose names were not recorded. Mihrî's story allows us to catch a glimpse of the unknown history of women. In the following pages, the discussion will focus on what it means to be an intellectual woman in her time and space through a consideration of the poetic discourse as another space in which Mihrî existed masterfully, allowing her to endure throughout the centuries.

PART TWO

Poetics of a Battlefield

5. An imagined scene of a female *meclis* in a picnic site. İstanbul University Library, T. 5502, "Zenannâme" (eighteenth century), fol. 78.

Since they say women lack reason
All their words should be excused.

But as for Mihrî, her well-wisher's supposition
As well as, what an intelligent person would say, is this:

A capable woman is much better than
A thousand incapable men.
A clear-headed woman is much better than
A thousand muddle-headed men.[1]

These illustrious lines by Mihrî Hatun appear in her "Tazarrunâme" (a humble prayer, petition), which is composed of 461 couplets in the form of a narrative and is found in her poetry collection.[2] She includes this long appeal at the end of her divan, after her other poems, which are examples from the usual genres, such as odes, lyrics, and quatrains. After performing the traditional expectations of what makes up a collection, she adds a poem that reflects her opinion about poetry and her place as a woman in the field of literature. It starts as a prayer, appearing to be a kind of repentance for being involved in the business of love (i.e., poetry). This kind of apology was common among poets and Mihrî seems to begin in the same way, but she also brings her gender into play. She praises the unity of Allah, his prophets and saints, and asks forgiveness for her rebelliousness. In the following lines, for example, she admits that she has committed sins and rebelled:

1. These lines are extracted from a section titled "Hâtime-yi Risâle" in Mihrî's poem, "Tazarrunâme." For a discussion of this section of the poem in detail, see Havlioğlu 2007. For the full poem in Latin script Ottoman Turkish, see Mihrî Hatun 2007, 351.

2. I have published the whole poem elsewhere (see Havlioğlu 2007).

The preacher's advice had no effect on me
I felt no bit of restraint in my heart

With all these sins, I turned to you for help
I am rebellious, you are generous, don't refuse me. (Mihrî Hatun 2007, 370; translation is my own)

The implication in these lines points to her involvement in poetry. With this poem, Mihrî makes use of the common poetic practice at the time of including appeals before or after poetry in the form of *sebeb-i telif* (reason for composition). This practice was particularly common after humorous or sexually explicit poems. However, what appears to be a declaration of appeal is in fact a statement about Mihrî's involvement in composing poetry as a woman. Mihrî takes this form and uses it to confirm that, though she may have sinned by being involved in poetry, she was a woman poet who was as good as a man.

In these lines Mihrî addresses the conception that "women lack reason"; that is, women were considered less capable in the intellectual fields. The statement is based on a *hadith* that appears in al-Bukhari's *Ṣaḥīḥ al-Bukhārī* collection. Al-Bukhari and al-Hajjaj are considered the authorities in the Islamic legal system because they established a way to determine the soundness of a *hadith*. They collected more than 10,000 *hadiths* that are considered absolutely true. The one that Mihrî addresses in this poem asserts that "women are deficient in reason and religion." It is especially popular among those who used it to prevent women's education and practice in the intellectual fields.

In the nineteenth century, Islamic feminists took issue with this *hadith*. Among them, Nazira Zeineddin (1908–76) contested its accuracy based on her dissection of its chain of authority. miriam cooke summarizes Zeineddin's discussions with her father on Islamic scriptures and the intricacies of the texts, writing that Zeineddin opposes the *hadith*, "women are deficient in reason," based on another saying of the Prophet Muhammad: "People lie about me. Whenever they say anything contradicting the Qur'an, I didn't say it. Any tradition that is not consonant with Qur'an is false. Whoever deliberately lies about me will find a place in hell" (cooke 2010, 32–38).

Zeineddin learned from her father how to debate with religious authorities on issues related to women. Even when the *hadith* is considered *sahih* (true), as in this case, Zeineddin proposed that it might not be true after all, by way of the very same discipline of tracing legitimacy used in the Islamic sciences. For Zeineddin, this *hadith* contradicts other sayings of the Prophet and the Qur'an, the only true authority for her.

Approximately four centuries before Zeineddin, Mihrî contested the same *hadith* by following another line of authority and raising a canonical poet as evidence. She inserts the line, "a capable woman is much better than a thousand incapable men," an appropriation of Sanai's line, "A good woman is better than a thousand men."[3] By alluding to a canonical poet, she not only makes a legitimate argument, but also shows the extent of her education and mastery of literature. She then emphasizes her argument with another similar line: "a clear-headed woman is much better than a thousand muddle-headed men." With these lines, she suggests that if women are essentially ignorant, they should be allowed to say whatever they like without bothering anybody. She seems to claim that intelligence is not an inherent quality of one's gender. As a woman who sets forth clear and sound arguments, she proves that women's ignorance is a false belief with no

3. Schimmel (1997, 20) discusses Sanai and quotes his well-known couplet, "A good woman is better than a thousand men."

reasonable explanation behind it. In other words, by composing these lines, she enacts her own point.

As Mihrî predicted, the above lines were noted and discussed at length in almost all of the early modern *tezkires*, as well as in modern anthologies. The proliferations of this *hadith* can be traced through the writings of Mihrî's successor, Ayşe Hubbî Hatun, who was well versed in the Islamic sciences. Ayşe Hubbî wrote the following lines, echoing those of Mihrî:

> Since you are one of the "deficient in wit"
> Your word need not be the most beautiful
> If the intellectual says no to what you say
> No woe be to you, it is he alone who errs
> This is the custom since this world began
> A person only and ever talks with peers
> Because in your time the talk of women is simple
> It is not equal to the sociability of men
> By this notion, if a superior should mingle with you
> It would be a point of pride for you and a shame for him
> Will the intellectual be harmed by this?
> If an accomplished one treats you as an equal. (Andrews and Kalpaklı 2005, 212)

This poem is quoted by Âşık Çelebi, and it clearly shares the perspective of Mihrî's earlier cited poem. An ode written in praise of Ayşe's institutional position at the palace also follows this same train of thought. It was written by the male poet Cinânî, who composed praises for another woman poet, Şemsiye Hatun, as well as for the *vâlide* sultans (the mothers of the sultans), such as Nurbanu Sultan and Safiye Sultan.[4] His

4. For a discussion of *kasides* written for women, see Havlioğlu and Aynur 2013.

poem to Ayşe Hubbî Hatun addresses the issue of women's intelligence:

> Her mental faculty with its maturity, would be enough for
> the world
> In her term, accusations such as women lack reason
> disappeared. (Havlioğlu and Aynur 2013, 96)

Cinânî's use of "women lack reason" reflects both Mihrî and Ayşe Hubbî's lines. Besides addressing this pervasive *hadith*, according to *tezkire* writers, Ayşe Hubbî consistently challenged degrading views of women, as in the following lines:

> Being feminine is no shame to the name of the sun
> Being masculine is no glory to the crescent moon.
> (Andrews and Kalpaklı 2005, 209)

Ayşe Hubbî's claim of equality between the two sexes is based on the difference between the gender of the Arabic name for the sun (*shams*), which is feminine, and the moon (*qamar*), which is masculine. To convince their readers of the legitimacy of a woman writer, biographers include a common saying in almost all *tezkires* about Mihrî: "A lion is a lion, isn't a female lion a lion too?"[5]

Overall, Mihrî's lines suggest the prejudice in the traditional discourse faced by women in the intellectual fields. Mihrî and Ayşe Hubbî, and even Zeineddin in the nineteenth century, demonstrate how they found the grounds on which to establish themselves as poets, writers, and intellectuals. Although they participate in the same discourse, they also find

5. For example, Âşık Çelebi uses this saying when he introduces Mihrî in his *Meşairü'ş-Şuarâ*. Derin Terzioğlu (1995) discusses a circumcision ceremony, told in narrative form, where a female performer is introduced with the help of the so-called saying.

a way to refuse or reject the bias against women. Their abilities and the acceptance they found came from their skill in pinpointing the glitches and gaps in the discourse. This way they could subvert the very discourse in which they were speaking. Using *hadith* or common sayings to their advantage was their way of portraying themselves as legitimate members of this elusive community and expressing their thoughts.

This poem mentioned above is a good example of such maneuvers in Mihrî's poetry. Her skillful moves were well calculated, allowing her to remain within the permissible limits of poetry while being critical of the poetic discourse. Her subversive use of poetic discourse not only allows her to insert her alternative subjective position, it also highlights a fundamental aspect of the discourse: its performativity. As poetic discourse is a rhetorical construction, it can be both performed and resisted. For this very reason, Mihrî was able to be a legitimate actor in the field of poetry while also being subversive. Her poems are sites of both existence and resistance, where she represents herself as a legitimate poet and discusses women's place in the literary arena.

4

Troubling Love

Performativity in Ottoman Poetry

To understand the ways in which Mihrî challenged the traditional discourse, a closer look is necessary. In a Butlerian framework, gender is constructed in linguistic formulations in the discourse in which it originated. In this sense, as Butler (1990, 24–25) defines performativity, it is not the conscious subject, but rather the discourse that makes the gender. The idea of performativity in language has been applied to classical Arabic poetry, primarily through J. L. Austin's speech act theory. Based on the performative function of language, speech act theory has proven useful for classical poetry, primarily for the Arabic ode (*qaṣīda*). The application of speech act theory to poetry unravels the deeper meanings of a poem, such as the direct relationship between an utterance and its effect. Moreover, as speech act theory works in an appropriate time and place through specific words and sentences, it helps to explain the historical background of poetry. A good example is Suzanne Stetkevych's (1993) use of the concept of gift exchange as a form of speech act for her reading of pre-Islamic *qaṣīda* poems. Analyzing poetry in light of its ceremonial aspects, Stetkevych's work suggests that, because it has immediate political and economic consequences like material exchange, classical Arabic poetry is performative. She argues that "the point, in terms of performative theory is not that the poems 'include' or 'describe' a request for ransom, but rather that the qasidah in toto, with all its conventions of structure, theme and motif is the ritual or ceremonial act of supplication that is a speech act" (107). Likewise, Beatrice Gruendler's (2010) reading of Abbasid poet Ibn al-Rumi (d. 896) suggests the interplay among words, acts, and contexts, as reflected in the relationship between the poet and the patron. The poet's demand translates into an economic currency that the patron feels obliged to bestow. Stefan Sperl and Yorgos Dedes's (2013) application of speech act theory alongside Gruendler's suggestions, which focus on speech uttered to rouse the target action, proves to be appropriate for their comparative reading of three Ottoman *kasîdes*. Sperl and Dedes's innovative reading of the three parallel poems confirms the pre-Islamic "root features" that are pervasive throughout the Islamicate literature in various regions and languages.

Within the framework of gender performativity and inspired by the application of speech act theory in pre-Islamic and classical Islamic poetry, I will try to investigate Mihrî's poems to trace her use of the poetic tradition to legitimate herself as a poet. Like all poets, Mihrî composed poetry for rewards, but she also did so to acquire acceptance in the poetic world. Besides her *kasîdes*, which evidently received monetary awards from the sovereign, her *gazels* were deliberately targeted to gain acceptance by the literary community. In her poems, Mihrî displays her desire to become a desiring subject as she uses the performativity of the tradition in subversive ways to accomplish her intent. In other words, there is a direct relationship between her use of poetic language and her desire to be accepted. She made certain choices that would allow her to become a legitimate member of the literary circles, such as challenging her male colleagues in poetic dialogues, in which she portrays herself as clearly different from them. As

Ann Rosalind Jones (1997, 371) puts it, "working out self-representations that challenge phallocentric discourses" can be a starting point to reading a woman poet. Self-representation, that is, a woman writer's negotiation and appropriation of the aesthetic discourse that she is writing in, appears both in her manipulation of the language as well as in the specific context that she situates herself.

A woman poet writing in a male tradition must go beyond expectations of her gender as she physically and conceptually enters forbidden territories, such as the *meclis* gathering or the writing of love lyrics. Even if she did not aspire to be different, the fact that her gender is excluded or despised in the dominant discourse of love will necessarily come into play. As she writes or speaks, she grapples with the discourse that preassigns silence to her gender role. She must adopt strategies to destabilize the gender system to exist as a speaking subject.

Mihrî's gender, as played out in her poetry, is the product of Ottoman poetic tradition and should be evaluated within this specific context. Poetry provides the physical and contextual space where gender is performed as a practice. Likewise, Mihrî's gendering process can be viewed not only through her poetry but also through the texts that discuss her. Therefore, I argue that Mihrî's gender as a woman and her potential for subversiveness can be found in her poetry through reading it alongside the Ottoman literary discourse, which was constructed in *meclis* gatherings. To delineate Mihrî's strategies of legitimation and subversion, it is necessary to situate Mihrî's poetry as a performance within its time and place.

As discussed in the previous chapters, in early modern Ottoman times, the two major features of the poetic discourse, spatial and aesthetic, could be considered obstacles for a woman poet. First, she would need to attend *meclises*, as the literature of this time was primarily practiced through performance in a literary space. Presumably, this would have been a challenge for a woman, as the Ottomans primarily adopted Islamic social practices, including gender segregation. Thus, we would not expect to see a respectable Muslim woman in a space where men were present. Second, the poetic aesthetics were constructed in such a way as to exclude women. A woman poet had to develop strategies to socialize in a male space while carving out an active speaker position in an aesthetic tradition of love in which all actors—both lover and beloved—were supposed to be men. Building on part 1, where I discussed the representation of women in a *meclis* culture, I will now turn to the aesthetic structure of poetry, that is, the discourse of love, and try to identify chasms in the tradition that allowed Mihrî to both legitimate herself and subvert it from within.

❀

Besides the poetic space—the *meclis* in the Ottoman Empire and the publishing world in Europe—a woman poet in early modern times had to face another major challenge: the discourse of love. As I mentioned earlier, love poems offered the possibility of a transgressive intervention for a woman poet because the conventions of love had been constructed for a male speaker. Ann Rosalind Jones (1990, 1) explains that, for European women poets, "the amorous discourses available to them (Roman elegy, pastoral, Neoplatonism, Petrarchism) had been constructed by male writers, who represented women as the silent objects of love rather than its active, articulate pursuers." As the language of high culture of the Renaissance was coded for a male speaker, women were excluded from the legitimate frameworks of expression. However, as Jones has shown in her research, women writers found ways to "negotiate" a space for themselves in the literary world. Although the Neoplatonic discourse did not view women favorably, women poets' adherence to it is understandable because without it they would not have been accepted as members of this high culture. The women poets' use of the same legitimate discourse, however, is the critical difference between a woman and a male writer: "When a member of the sex systematically excluded from literary performance takes a dominant/hegemonic position toward an approved discourse, she is, in fact, destabilizing the gender system that prohibits her claim to public language—although with limited disturbance to that system" (Jones 1990, 2). What seems to be an imitation is women poets' appropriation of the discourse of love and their negotiation of a space in the literary world. Similarly, Mihrî, as an Ottoman woman poet, had to confront the discourse of love.

In terms of the construction of love in the Ottoman literary tradition, comparative discussions of the Neoplatonic ideals of love and Islamic mysticism have shown that the two share the dual concept of the exoteric and esoteric worlds as foundational concepts. As Sperl and Dedes (2013, 198) discuss, "what they have in common is the notion that all manifestations of material reality carry within themselves the imprint of the heavenly power which brought them into existence. Thus according to the Qur'an, every created object is a 'sign', an āya (Tk. âyet), pointing to the Creator." The major difference between Neoplatonism and Islamic mysticism, as Sperl and Dedes (2013, 199) assert, is the Neoplatonic "hierarchy of mirroring analogies which stretches in an unbroken chain from the lowliest of creatures to the angelic spheres and ultimately to the One who is the source of all." Mystical Islam conceptualizes "the One" as the unity of all and true existence as the combination of the material and spiritual worlds, which are not opposites, but parts of a whole. The reality of these polarized worlds—material and spiritual, worldly and heavenly, or this world and that world—is known to some people who are responsible for hiding this secret. Walter Andrews (1985) refers to this group as the "spiritual elite" who showed the symbolic truth to the masses of humanity.

Poets and artists were thought to have represented the truth in their works. The polarity between the material and spiritual worlds constitutes the basis for ambiguity in poetry as an aesthetic value. Annemarie Schimmel's explanation of religious and worldly poetry, based on the complementary nature of the exoteric and esoteric realms, points to the ideals of Islamic mystical aesthetics: "Thus poetry provides almost unlimited possibilities for creating new relations between worldly and other-worldly images, between religious and profane ideas; the talented poet may reach a perfect interplay of both levels and make even the most profane poem bear a distinctly religious flavor" (quoted in Andrews 1985, 63). The abstract nature of poetry is not a restriction; on the contrary, it is an opportunity to add layers of meaning. A good poet can make use of this feature to communicate his/her message.

The poet's ability to connect the two worlds can be considered a talent. As the Qur'an shows, each entity is an *āya*, a sign or a microcosm in this world, which represents the macrocosm. Thus, a good representation is a reminder of this truth. If an artwork achieves this, it is considered good. As Behrens-Abouseif (1999, 26) suggests, for al-Ghazali, "pleasure is a form of cognition" and "to enjoy is to know." Therefore, people enjoy recognizing something they already know in their heart. The poem or a piece of art is beautiful as it can achieve this form of cognition, triggering pleasure. A very common Ottoman literary tool, *telmîh* (allusion), is a good example of this unspoken agreement between the artist and the audience as the basis for creating and appreciating beauty. As I have discussed elsewhere, the poet invokes the feeling of a shared world between herself and the audience, and the way she does that is closely related to her literary choices (Havlioğlu 2015a). For instance, classical love stories, such as Leylâ and Mecnûn or Yusuf and Züleyhâ, are some of the sources used by Ottoman poetry. Poets often allude to these stories by mentioning a word or a phrase—such as the well of Yusuf or the youth of Züleyhâ—to suggest the suffering one has to endure to reach the beloved and the reward one could get in the end. Because they know the story, the audience understands the clue. Each poet refers to a different version or part of a story and this choice points to his or her specific intent.

Ambiguity as an artistic value is at the heart of Islamicate poetry. The poet's intentions are not to clearly define, but rather to imply the purpose of the artwork to remind the audience of what they already know. In this framework, the beloved represents ideal beauty without having any specific description. For instance, the gender-neutral, third-person pronoun in Turkish works well with the gender ambiguity of the beloved. Moreover, the lover's gender, even though he is almost always male, is fluid contingent to the role he plays in poetry. The lover and the beloved continuously change roles to be active or passive. Although the lover seems to be all powerful because he controls the narrative, the beloved torments him by not giving him what he wants in all silence. Through the change of roles and exchanging control, they are in a perpetual play of desire. The beloved does not have clear physical characteristics other than hyperbolic qualities: a swaying body, a moon-like face, and arrow-like eyelashes that kill with a glance. The beloved is an idea rather than a real-life body. The mystical dimension of Islamicate aesthetics identifies beauty as the representation of God and his creation. As Behrens-Abouseif (1999, 26) explains, it is an "inward beauty which is perceived by the 'eye of the heart.'" To find it, one must contemplate God and his creations. Unlike Aristotle's idea of mimesis, Islamic philosophers do not offer a formula for the composition of artistic beauty. As there is no way to identify God's beauty with the physical qualities of this world, the Islamic arts do not seek mimesis. The intention is never to recreate something that already exists before our eyes. The artists' goal, instead, is to construct an experience for the spectators or listeners that reminds them of the ideal; that is, the beauty in the world that can only be seen with the heart's eye.

Putting aside aesthetic theories, however, poetry has a direct link with real life. Although it can be read as a meditation on the beauty of God, it can also reflect the poet's experiences. The richness and value of a poem lie behind its layers of meaning. The representation of the beloved in this world is the prepubescent boy.[1] In terms of aesthetics, the age of the beloved is crucially important here. One of the aspects of the beloved's beauty is his peach-fuzz facial hair, which is traditionally described as a green line (*ḫatt*). As the facial hair appears darker on his face, he is no longer considered as beautiful and is disqualified as an object of desire. Despite the references to his body, it is difficult to define his gender using modern vocabulary. The simple female/male binary does not explain the complex construction of the beloved's gender. Among many factors, age and its relation to reproductivity had significant importance. The prepubescent/presexual and the elderly/postsexual were similarly treated as gender neutral. In other words, gender was not a fixed category but was ever-changing according to one's biological development. Although this was not related to sexual preference and desire, it made a difference in terms of regulating society.

1. For a discussion on Ottoman beloveds, see Andrews and Kalpaklı 2005, 38–42; in Iranian history, see Najmabadi 2005, 11–25.

For instance, Leslie Peirce's (1993, ix) study of the Ottoman imperial harem demonstrates that sexuality was controlled in accordance with age for both men and women. Whereas for a young man, growing a beard was a claim of manhood, for an elderly woman, aging beyond childbearing years could be an advantage because it meant less restriction on her life. Peirce further suggests that a woman reached her peak of power as she aged and lost her reproductive capabilities.

In terms of the intellectual world, Khaled el-Rouayheb (2005, 13) suggests that pederasty was a common practice and that gender distribution among learned men was hierarchical in terms of seniority. In the homosocial world of poetry, where the lover/poet was almost always an adult man, his counterpart in the business of love, the beloved, was a younger and voiceless man. Though for males, gender was fluid and hierarchical, the poetic world's doors were closed to the female sex. In this framework, "male" was not seen as a fixed category, but as a process based on performance and age. Likewise, as Andrews and Kalpaklı (2005, 37) have suggested, "the beloved is ambiguously gendered on the surface with a strong bias towards the masculine." There are a few exceptions, such as Azîzî and Enderûnlu Fâzıl's narrative poems, where the beloveds were explicitly women. However, Enderûnlu Fâzıl felt the need to explain his work *Zenannâme* (the book of women), a commissioned work that places women in the role of the beloved: he wrote it, without conviction, to please his patron.

Focusing on the Arabic poetry of the Ottoman lands in the early modern period, El-Rouayheb (2005, 34) confirms that beauty also appeared in the male form in Arabo-Islamic aesthetics. Moreover, while the mystical interpretation of poetry conceptualizes love between the lover and the beloved as a spiritual act and the male lover/poet's desire for the beloved as yearning for unity with God, this kind of poetry could also be an example of profane love. The best examples of the beloved depicted as an attractive young postpubescent man appear in the *şehrengîz* (city thriller) genre. These poems chronicle the male beauties of the city as one of the urban attractions. As Andrews and Kalpaklı (2005, 90) suggest, by the end of the sixteenth century, poetry had been accused of being too worldly as "it became unusually fashionable, especially among the Ottoman economic and intellectual elites (but not exclusively) to become more or less publicly enamored of beautiful young men, certain of whom became quite famous." In this framework, as Mihrî was composing her poems, poetry was becoming an entirely male space that excluded women both spatially and conceptually.

Putting aside the common understanding that the beloved in Ottoman poetry was an androgynous beauty, the poet or lover was clearly associated with manliness and held either the controlling/active or subservient/passive roles. As discussed earlier, male poets are overwhelmingly dominant in number in biographical dictionaries. Regardless, in the context of the discourse of love, Ottoman poetry was primarily a male culture. The traditional discourse of love, based on the assumption that both the speaker/poet and the beloved are male, automatically excludes women. It is a system in which all actors are male and that eschews romantic connection between a man and a woman. Even when the beloved was a real person, such as a sultan or a patron, rather than a metaphor for God, the poet maintained his male gender.

As a poet, the challenge Mihrî posed to the field of poetry stemmed from the foundational structure of the aesthetic system and the gender identification of poethood, traditionally characterized as manly (*merdâne*) and the men of the battlefield (*merd-i meydân*). Poets, who were overwhelmingly male in number, presented this gendered quality as a necessary aspect of their art. Thus, if a woman was to become a poet, she would have to perform manliness or defy this expectation and be excluded from the world of poetry. Because Mihrî addresses this issue in her poetry, we can assume that it was one of the primary obstacles she had to confront as a poet. Her strategy, however, was not to ignore or to defy the classification. Instead, she challenged manliness and its association with the male biology. By embracing the values of manliness, such as courage and fearlessness, she claimed it as a woman and, by doing so, challenged the traditional gender construction of Ottoman poetry.

Etymologically, manliness (*erlik* or *merdlik*) is a positive quality associated with the male gender. It means courage, endurance, and morality. Womanliness (*zen* or *zenlik*), on the other hand, is considered to be its binary counterpart. It is associated with worldliness and temporality. The poet is expected to be manly, that is, courageous and brave on the battlefield of poetry. He needs to fight against the temptation and dangers of this world, such as destiny, time, and fortune, all of which are represented by women and work against the artist. The woman reminds him of the nature of this world and its associations such as time, temptations, and mortality. As he attains the spiritual world, he must give up everything the woman symbolizes. The following is some of the vocabulary that *tezkire* writers used for poets: *merdâne*, *âşıkâne*, and *muhannesâne* for manliness and, in terms of his orientation, he is either *mahbûbperest*, the male beloved worshiper, and/or *zenperest*, the female beloved worshiper.

In the *tezkire* writers' representation of Mihrî as a poet, the vocabulary of manliness and womanliness coexist. Latîfî (2000, 510) defined Mihrî's writing as both womanly and manly. He clearly defines manliness as a quality that allows men to engage in love. By love, he means either spiritual contemplation or erotic engagement with the prepubescent male beloved. He defines Mihrî's handwriting and mannerisms as womanly; however, in the business of love, she is courageous enough to chase beloveds so she is therefore manly. From this we can deduce that, for Latîfî, her womanliness is only in her physical script—by implication, her body. Her gestures and behavior as a lover/poet, however, make her manly.

Based on his discussion of Mihrî as a poet, Latîfî defines the composition of poetry as manly. It is no surprise, then, that he uses *merdâne* for manliness, but also adds *âşıkâne*, meaning "in the manner of a lover," to the list of qualities of a poet. It follows that, in the context of poetry, the ability to engage in love is a positive quality of manliness, one that is explicitly attributed to men. When a woman poet entered the fray, *tezkire* writers revealed a kind of gender complexity, as is apparent in Âşık's entry on Mihrî. As discussed in part 1 in detail, Âşık uses rather confusing expressions, such as *yusuf kızlığı* (virginity of Yusuf) to define Mihrî's virginity and *hayz-ı ricâl* (menstrual fluid of men) to define obscenely sexual writings as polluting, the way menstrual fluid is supposed to be for women.

Âşık, following Latîfî's formula, begins with similar terminology and defines Mihrî in comparable ways, as seen in the following: "her writing is like a woman's embroidery, and her composition is whorish" (Âşık Çelebi 2010, 623–24). Like Latîfî, he refers to her writing as womanly, using the phrase "woman's embroidery." We do not know for certain if Mihrî did so herself, but women in Islamic societies have always been involved in calligraphy, particularly in the field of *tezyîn*, the decoration of calligraphy. In contrast with her beautiful script, her composition is depicted as *rûspiyâne*, literally meaning whorish. Âşık also calls her a female beloved, *mahbûbe*, and a male-beloved worshipper, *mahbûbperest* or *şâhidbazlık*, stating that she was in the business of love. In the context of love, then, she was manly. Âşık also adds *merd-i meydân*, man of the battlefield, to the list of vocabulary associated with poetry.

In such a homogeneous male system, a woman poet has few chances to overcome her marginalization. Her gender determines her destiny as an outsider. She may somehow succeed in entering the *meclis*, but to become a poet/lover she must perform the role of the poet, which is necessarily manly. Because she expressed herself as a manly woman within the discourse of poetry, Mihrî was a marginal poet. As she demonstrates, though, this marginal position does not have to be a negative trait. It is her subject position in a Kristevan sense; by simply being clear about her gender as a woman and doing something unexpected, such as composing love poetry for the beloved, she causes a rupture. When she uses this prestigious language and enters the literary space as a woman, it is no longer the same language or space. In this way, her marginal position works as an advantage for her; while legitimating her poetry, it also allows her to subvert the dominant discourse from within. Her revolutionary potential is at the core of her marginality and engagement with men as a female poet/lover. It allows her to insert herself as a legitimate, but also an alternative, lover. The subversion happens naturally, as it stems from the essence of her position as a woman poet—not a beloved—within the dominant discourse of love. Therefore, she did not change anything else about the discourse. For example, she did not try to represent a female homosocial discourse by presenting a female beloved. I believe that the poetic tradition draws a clear line for the depiction of beauty and, to remain legitimate, she never crossed that line. Rather, she consistently challenged the male qualities of poethood and showed how a woman can be manly, too.

This unique example of a legitimate and celebrated woman poet crystalizes the gender construction of poetry. As Mihrî performs as a poet, the male tradition is confronted. We can no longer avoid dealing with gender based on the common misconception that it has no role in Ottoman poetry. In fact, the performativity of Ottoman poetic discourse is all about gender. Mihrî's marginal existence as a woman shows that poetry is a male field. Her marginality is an artifact of the dominant discourse and it defines her revolutionary role in the poetic world. Moreover, because she insists on taking up a male role as a woman and playing by the legitimate rules (e.g., producing in certain genres, rhymes, vocabulary, and with certain topoi), she confirms that poetry is performative. By following its rules, one can be legitimate or, by stretching its limits, one can be transgressive. After grounding herself as a poet, she carefully chose tools from the tradition to introduce her self-representation as an active female lover. In this way, she was able to be both subversive and accepted as a woman.

I explore Mihrî's subversiveness in the following pages by discussing her poetry vis-à-vis the dominant poetic discourse. I examine two cases in which she competed with her male colleagues to show her legitimacy as a woman poet. Instead of resisting the discourse, she found ruptures from within and transformed her role as a woman poet. The first case is her parallel poems written for the celebrity poet of her time, Necâtî. In these poems, she performs one of the classic exercises, writing parallel poems (*nazîres*) to another accepted poet's works, to show off her skills. While doing that as a woman, she had to redefine the "manliness" of the poet. The second case is her poetic dialogue with a fellow poet from the same court in Amasya. Her responses to Makâmî's poems, which come across as advances of love, are eye-opening. As Makâmî puts her in the place of the beloved and asks for a kiss, he not only risks his reputation as a poet but also as a man (because she is a manly woman). With the use of a classic tool such as humor, she reminds him of their roles in the poetic world.

5

Performance and Legitimacy

Necâtî and Mihrî

They say your rival boasts and says, "I'll kill her one day"
If he's a man, let him come and I'll show manliness to
that unmanly coward[1]

In these lines, Mihrî sets up a traditional love triangle between the lover/poet, the beloved, and the rival. After hearing the rival's threats to kill her, she challenges him/her with an invitation to fight on the battlefield of poetry. In the discourse of love, each player has a specific role in constructing the unattainable union. While the silent beloved torments the yearning lover, who holds the only speaking subject position, the rival competes with the lover for the beloved's attention. There is another significant role for the rival, however, relating to the tension between the inner circle of the literary community and the outsiders. The rival represents the orthodox religious community, which does not approve of the mystical ideas and lifestyles of the poetic world. Therefore, the rival can be both an admirer of the beloved and a pious challenger. Walter Andrews (1985, 162) explains the external role of the rivals as the "oppositions to the basic functions of the party: on the

1. See appendix, poem no. 22.

one hand to the love/alcohol obsessions, and on the other hand to the emotional/mystical interpretation of the party behavior." When poets stand behind the ideas of the poetic world, their legitimacy and acceptance in poetic circles are constructed through their poetic performance, where they advocate for their people.

In this framework, the couplet demonstrates Mihrî's claim for her inclusion in the poetic circles. To do so, she adopts the courageous voice of the poet as a way to prove herself. She shows that she can fight like a man with the rival who is, within literary standards, unmanly. As is clear in the *tezkire* writers' discourse, courage is considered one of the manifestations of poethood, both of which are traditionally attributed to the male gender. We should, then, consider the reason for courage to be a requirement in the field of poetry. Being a poet means choosing a path that diverges from the morally accepted or orthodox religious ways of living. Therefore, manliness is equal to poethood, as the poet lives by the rules of love: the mystical interpretations of religion, literature, and lifestyle. Although the rival may be a man, because he does not belong to the literary community, he cannot be considered manly. Manliness does not inherently belong to the male gender; rather, because poets were almost always men, it happened to be historically claimed by men. In being claimed by a woman, based on her skills as a poet, it can also legitimately belong to a woman. As discussed in the previous chapter, Âşık Çelebi noted in his entry for Mihrî that she was much more manly than many men. Âşık implicitly mentions the unmanly male poets who did not fit in the literary circles for one reason or another.

As in the case of this couplet, in her poetry, Mihrî demonstrates that the way for a woman to claim manliness was through performing poetry. Her strategy is not to defy the traditional rules; on the contrary, she embraces the values attached to poethood. What she does is subtler, but eye-opening. While she carefully selects actions that highlight her belonging in the intellectual field, she confronts the traditional gender construction. Although she uses the same poetic discourse, she does not imitate her male colleagues. On the contrary, she challenges the system with her subversive use of it. For instance, by claiming the positive values of manliness attributed to a poet as a woman, values traditionally associated with men, she redefines these gender values. In her woman's voice, the battlefield of poetry and its vocabulary no longer have the same meaning, but are reconstructed in a whole new way. Moreover, when we consider the poems as oral performances in the physical environment of a *meclis*, the effect must have been unsettling.

In the following discussion, I will focus on a case in which Mihrî entered into poetic dialogues with her colleague Necâtî. In her parallel poems, there is a clear difference between her male colleagues' use of the poetic tradition and her own. Her competing poems with Necâtî point out those qualities of a poet typically associated with men and the way in which Mihrî resisted this assumption as a woman. In these poems, her voice is persuasive and insistent through her identification with Züleyhâ, a classical female character in the poetic tradition who exhibited manly qualities as a woman.

Poet as a Man, Poet as a Woman: Necâtî and Mihrî

Among the common practices and rites of passage for Ottoman poets was the composition of *nazîres* to celebrated poets. To write a proper parallel poem, the poet had to adhere to certain rules. The parallel poem had to follow the same meter, rhyme scheme, and refrain words. Furthermore, it might follow the same imagery and themes. Within the very limited space left for invention, poets managed to recycle poetry and create new meanings. The long-lived tradition of writing parallel poems was something all poets of this period attempted to perform. It was a recognition and appreciation of the tradition, as well as a display of mastery.[2] Nonetheless, it was also a competition to show who excelled in the business of love and could produce better poetry. Like other poets, Mihrî wrote *nazîres*. These allowed her to enter into poetic discussions so as to demonstrate her skills as a poet. Among her *nazîres*, the ones written to the poet Necâtî (d. 1509), a celebrated poet of the time, are particularly significant for my discussion.

Necâtî's real name was İsa or Nuh and, according to stories in the *tezkires*, he was first the slave of a woman in the city of Edirne (Çavuşoğlu 1971, 6). Later, his owner adopted him as her son and he was emancipated. Thanks to his skills in poetry, he eventually arrived at the palace in Istanbul. Necâtî is a prime example of how anyone could be a poet, even a former slave. As far as we know, he did not receive a *medrese* education, but he performed poetry according to its rules and aligned himself with notable people. He was very close friends with Müeyyedzâde, Mihrî's friend and mentor. In the preface of his divan, Necâtî mentions Müeyyedzâde as a great patron of poetry and states that, were it not for him, he would not have been able to finish his work. This, in addition to the fact that Âşık Çelebi was Müeyyedzâde's grandson, can explain the detailed accounts of Mihrî and her poetic competition with Necâtî in the *tezkires*. Regardless, Necâtî was one of the most accomplished poets and any poet would have wanted to compose like him. He was one of the most referenced poets of the early modern period.

2. For further information on the *nazîre* tradition, see Kalpaklı 2006.

Although she wrote many parallels to his poems, there is no poem in Necâtî's divan that acknowledges Mihrî's name. If we return to the *tezkires*, however, we see that they all enjoyed commenting on this issue. Apparently, like the story of İskender, they found Mihrî's competition with Necâtî significant, if not amusing. As with other issues, such as her love affairs or speculation about her virginity, *tezkire* writers made conflicting remarks about Necâtî's supposed reaction to Mihrî's poems. They quote the following parallel poem in particular:

> She delicately censured Necâtî, saying [in response to the following]:
>
> > So let there not be a single bit of benevolence in earth or sky
> > For mattress and covering a reed-mat is enough for Necâtî
>
> Mihrî said:
>
> > O Necâtî, if you want a reed mat to lie on
> > For Mihrî, just a place on the beloved's threshold is enough (Âşık Çelebi 2010, 623–24; translation my own)

Because Mihrî wanted to be an accepted poet, she may have written parallel poems to prove that she was as talented as Necâtî. Within the poetic discourse, being a poet meant being a lover, one whose only desire was to unite with the beloved. In the abovementioned lines, she competes with Necâtî, who states in his poem that all he needs is a reed mat on the beloved's threshold. Mihrî, on the other hand, tries to defeat him with her refusal of any comforts, including a reed mat. A simple space is enough for her.

According to the *tezkires*, Necâtî said the following lines in response to Mihrî's parallel poems:

> You, who write parallels to my poetry
> Beware of veering from the path of modesty.
>
> Don't say, "Look here, in meter and rhyme
> My poem is the equal to Necâtî's.
>
> In both the [Ottoman] words are in three letters
> Are "shame" and "skill" in truth the same? (Latîfî 2000, 510; translation my own)

In the Arabic script, the words for shame, *ayb* (*ayıb*), and talent, *hnr* (*hüner*), are both written in three letters. This poem could have been a warning to Mihrî. Apparently, Necâtî was not happy that she was writing poems parallel to his own. Considering Latîfî and Âşık's need to explain her inclusion in the world of poetry, a woman poet is not a natural member of the intellectual circles. Therefore, Necâtî's reaction makes sense. Because he existed within the same discourse used in the *tezkires*, being a male poet, Necâtî would have been expected to react this way to a woman poet. Even if Necâtî enjoyed her interest in his poetry, he would have felt the need to make such a rhetorical complaint at the implied comparison between an aspiring woman poet and a celebrated male poet, such as himself. However, it is worth keeping in mind that neither this poem nor the following appear in Necâtî's divan:

> One day a clever fellow among Necâtî's conversational companions asked him, "Necâtî Bey, which of our arts of poetry do you like best?" that eloquent personage and prince of speech replied, intending wit and double meaning, "It is a poetess of sweet conceits who likes your ambiguities and desires of conversation":

O Mihrî your being in the world is a wellspring of conceits
Now the poets of the age praise you. (Latîfî 2000, 510; translation my own)

In this passage, Latîfî admits that, as an accepted poet, Mihrî's poems were in fact honoring Necâtî. As I will discuss in the following pages, Necâtî was one of the clear male voices of his time. From the perspective of the rules of aesthetic discourse, Necâtî's use of a manly voice is not surprising. However, a comparison of his use of it and her own will help us to understand Mihrî's subversive use of this discourse. After a brief overview of Necâtî's claims to manliness, I will turn to Mihrî's poetry, in which she performs within the same discourse, but with a nuanced difference.

As is clear from *tezkire* writers' definitions, a poet was expected to be manly and ready for combat in the arena of poetry. Further proof for this can be found in Necâtî's poetry, as his self-representation highlights his manliness as a poet. Table 3 illustrates the frequency of manliness terms used in lyric poems by Necâtî and Mihrî. When compared to the total number of words they used in their poems (Necâtî 138,820 and Mihrî 58,638), 0.06 percent of Necâtî's and 0.01 percent of Mihrî's total words are related to manliness.

The terms representing manliness in table 3 were first collected from *tezkires* and then searched for in the poetry of Necâtî and Mihrî. According to the numbers collected after searching all of their *gazels*, and after adjusting these numbers with the total number of words in their poems, Necâtî used the terms six times more than Mihrî. Mihrî never calls herself a man, whereas Necâtî does; for that reason, she barely uses words such as *âdem*, *er*, or *merd*. However, she does mention *merdâne*, or manliness, more often, as she refers to engagement in love.

TABLE 3

Vocabulary Referring to Maleness in the Poetry of Mihrî and Necâtî

Poet	*No. Appearances*						
	Âdem	*Er*	*Erlik*	*Merd*	*Merdâne*	*Nâmerd*	*Total*
Necâtî	63	16	1	5	6	0	91
Mihrî	5	1	1	1	2	1	11

In addition to the frequency of their use of these words, the context in which they were used is critical for a comparison of the two poets. For this reason, I will discuss some examples of their use of these manliness terms in their poetry. The following couplet is extracted from a poem by Necâtî as an example of his self-perception as a man:

> Necâtî, aren't you a man? Don't give in to this world.
> While it [the world] is a woman, in such form, it never
> submits to a man. (Necâtî 1963, *gazel* no. 449;
> translation my own)

Here, Necâtî reminds himself that he is a man, so he should resist this "womanly" world. Like a woman, the material world is a temptation for a man, who proves himself by the measure of his resistance. In other words, the world is a woman and a man cannot change it. He is presented with two options: he either gives in to her or he resists her and retains his manliness. In this context, women represent danger and temptation for men. Men, conversely, manifest themselves by their own resistance. This idea of the dangerous woman and the vulnerable man is similar to the story of Yusuf and Züleyhâ. One of the many temptations Yusuf had to resist was Züleyhâ's love. This story is instrumental in understanding the concepts of man and woman in Ottoman poetry.

The following couplet echoes this idea of resistance as a masculine quality, acquired by a man:

> What a woman this world is, so be pure in deed and honest
> Like a man, my beloved darling Necâtî, like a man.
> (Necâtî 1963, *gazel* no. 564; translation my own)

These lines clearly attribute a certain quality to manliness: integrity. As a woman, the world is corrupt. The following lines make a further assertion about women:

> Hands off, if you have divorced the woman of this world
> O Necâtî, a person should be a man of his word. (Necâtî 1963, *gazel* no. 638; translation my own)

Necâtî advises himself that he must divorce the world and he does so by imitating the actual divorcing ritual in saying it three times. He uses the verbs *boşamak*, meaning "to divorce," and *el çekmek*, meaning "to withdraw one's hand from," for leaving the woman of this world. He is withdrawing from this world as a mystic and in this case the world with all its deceits and illusions is portrayed as a woman. As a man of his word, once he has divorced this world he should not be tempted into relations with it. These are things that poets, and human beings in general, should resist to return to the world of spirituality. In these lines, Necâtî reminds himself that he promised he would give up on this world, that is, give up on worldliness. In the second line, he uses the idiom *sözinün eri*, or "man of his word," to refer to himself as an honest man. The idiom is a good example of the dominant discourse, which viewed honesty and trustworthiness as male qualities. Furthermore, there is no idiom, such as a "woman of her word," that connotes integrity as a female quality.

The last two couplets are among the rare cases in which women came into the discussion. Necâtî uses *zen* for "woman" and *zen-i zemâne* for the "woman of the times." In these instances, "woman" has a negative connotation and is used as a comparison with manliness—a comparison that is always in favor of manliness. Interestingly, Mihrî never refers to women or femaleness in her poetry. She does not make a comparison between men and women. Both Mihrî and Necâtî composed their poetry within the traditional discourse, in which a bias toward the male gender was ingrained. It was expected from any poet, man or woman, to use this discourse to produce poetry considered to be legitimate. Likewise, the following examples demonstrate that the discourse of manliness was pervasive throughout Ottoman literary history.

Revânî (d. 1523/1524) was another of Mihrî's contemporaries. He was also awarded with monetary gifts by Bayezid II, but he thrived during the reign of Selim I (1512–20). The following couplet is an example of his take on manliness:

> O Revânî, like lovers on the battlefield of love
> Haven't you seen manly men who give up their lives
> (Revânî 1986, *gazel* no. 36; translation my own)

Similarly, the following couplet belongs to one of the most celebrated poets, Bâkî (d. 1600), who lived about fifty years later.

> O Bâkî whoever has a weakness for the old woman of this world is not a male
> The manly men on the path of love don't call him a man.
> (Küçük 1994, *gazel* no. 304; translation my own)

These examples show how, throughout the history of Ottoman poetry, poethood was associated with men and the wretched world with women. Because Mihrî was aware of the ways in which her gender was conceptualized, she purposefully resisted it in her poetry.

As a method of resistance, Mihrî not only avoided referring to women, but also chose to explore a different meaning of manliness, associating it with those qualities she valued without giving up her female gender. When Mihrî defined herself as manly, she reconfigured the word so that it no longer referred only to men. In essence, the quality of manliness encompasses resistance, courage, and fearlessness. By doing this as a woman, she both redefined the word and explicitly attributed it to herself.

In the following poem, Mihrî declares herself to be among the lovers who are defined as manly within the poetic discourse:

> We are among those who came to sacrifice our lives for the beloved's sake
> We have become the seekers after pain, among those who came for a cure
>
> We are among those who came manfully to the playing field of love
> That might make my head a ball for the mallet of your love locks.[3]

By using the "we" pronoun in these lines, Mihrî explicitly includes herself in the group of poets, implying that she has the same qualities as the other members of this group. In the first couplet, Mihrî shows her understanding of poethood or of being a lover as a courageous act. This depiction of lovers also applies to artists in general; they are extraordinary people living on the margins of society. Their measure of creativity is equated with the courage they need to survive. Mihrî, as a woman who survives in an arena that is not supposed to include her, places herself among that group of people who

3. See appendix, poem no. 20.

resist restrictions. As she, too, struggles, she is also manly in this way. She uses the plural "we" to emphasize this group identity. The following is the last couplet from the same poem:

> O Mihrî, for the candle of the beloved's cheek, always
> Let me burn like a moth, for I am among those who came on fire

The image of the lover as a moth drawn to the flame of the beloved's beauty or cheek is a traditional one to describe the condition of the lover. As Mihrî is ready to burn like a moth, she is among the (manly) poets. This is a community of poets who are fearless in expressing their commitment to the art of love. The following couplets from a different poem by Mihrî confirm the manly qualities of a poet:

> If you are a lover, leave your virtue and modesty aside for love's sake
> Strive on this path, give your life to it, else you will lose the beloved.
>
> O help! If you are manly, it is time to strive and drive off the rival
> Exert yourself that the thorn not grasp the fresh rose's skirt.[4]

For lovers or poets, social values such as virtue and modesty are not applicable, since their job defies these conventions. Being a lover is the job of a poet, but this requires courage, as the poet must ignore social values. Here, Mihrî defines the role of *merd*, a man, as parallel to that of a lover. By playing with the idea of fighting and hunting, she implies that poetry

4. See appendix, poem no. 21.

is a battlefield. These are all traditional definitions of manliness and poetry.

Mihrî's reception was presumably related to the fact that manliness, although historically used to refer to men, is performative. As this was a male-dominated world, the language reflected its rulers. Consequently, all positive human attributes, such as courage and reason, were attributed to men. This did not mean that all men, simply because they were physically male, could be manly. Thus, Mihrî could make the argument in her poetry that she was more manly than those who did not have her courage and reason.

Mihrî demonstrated, both through her poetry and her personal life, that she could be as good of a poet as any male poet and that being a poet does not require one to be a man. Instead, it requires understanding and courage to take up the discourse of love. In her poetry, she defined the true meaning of manliness as reason, courage, spirituality, and the ability to control one's desires. Her courage as a poet was evident in the ways in which she competed in the poetic arena. In her parallel poems to Necâtî, she managed to create a debate in the poetic circles, as seen in the *tezkires*. As an educated and brave woman, Mihrî did not fit into the stereotypical definition of woman as cunning, dangerous, material, sexual, and temporal. Mihrî's technique for inserting herself, as a woman, into the traditional discourse was well calculated. By claiming manliness as a woman, she deconstructed the binary gender construction of the Ottoman poetic discourse and redefined the genders through poetry.

Claim of Poethood/Lover as a Woman

Ottoman poetry has traditionally been defined as a strict structure comprised of conventions that do not allow any poet, man or woman, to reflect their own self-identification. However, this traditional reading of poetry fails to distinguish the difference between the two fundamental aspects of poetry: structure and context. The classical structure is fundamentally organized and does not allow much alteration. However, there are literary tools that allow poets to communicate different meanings in context. For instance, poets signed their poems with a *mahlas* that referred to the persona that they hoped to create through their poetry. These pen names are a type of self-representation. Moreover, the particular words poets used to identify themselves are also an indication of personal choice. A good example of this is Necâtî's reference to himself as a *yetim*, or orphan, in his poems. According to *tezkire* writers, he was an orphan; therefore, in this case, his self-representation was accurate and specific to himself (Âşık Çelebi 2010, 850). Poets may each mean something different with their words when choosing the vocabulary available in the poetic discourse according to their specific needs. Though they used the same poetic discourse, each poet may mean something different.

In the following discussion, I focus on a case in which Mihrî composed a poem parallel to one by Necâtî, demonstrating a clear difference between the use of the poetic tradition by her male colleague and herself. In Necâtî's poem, he associates the qualities of a poet with being a man, whereas Mihrî resists this presumption as a woman. In these poems, her voice is persuasive and insistent through her self-identification with Züleyhâ. Because using classical characters in poetry was a common practice, both Mihrî and Necâtî incorporated them into their poems with a similar frequency. In terms of their use of female characters, Mihrî not only used them more often than Necâtî, but she also contextualized them as active lovers. This is an indication of her personal choice within her poetry, yet it is more meaningful when we look at the way she used these characters in context. I will try to illustrate how she manipulated the discourse of love by analyzing the parallel poem by Mihrî and Necâtî with the refrain word of *sana*, "to you."

Before I begin my close reading of these poems, it is important to know the background story of Necâtî's poem, which was recorded by Âşık Çelebi. According to Âşık Çelebi (2010, 850), Necâtî originally wrote this poem to draw the attention of Sultan Mehmed II. He wrote the poem on a piece of paper, rolled it up, and placed it in the turban of Yorgi, one of the sultan's companions. While Yorgi was playing chess with the sultan, Mehmed noticed this piece of paper, took it out of the turban, and read it. He liked the poem and appointed Necâtî as his secretary. Because of this poem, Necâtî acquired one of the best positions available for a poet at the time. This incident is not extraordinary, though. Poets often competed with one another to get the attention of the sultan, or some other powerful patron, through poetry. This story not only reflects a common practice of the time, it also highlights my previous comments about poetry as performance. Necâtî knew how to play the game by its rules and, for this reason, received a great reward.

The poem by Necâtî:

1. What can we do? The sigh of early morning has no
   effect on you
   My dear friend, perhaps God will grant a sense of justice
   to you

2. The conversation with wine will be pleasant on a
   moonlit night
   Come to the gathering and scatter light, for the name
   "moon" we give to you

3. What can we do, if fate offers to you sweet drink and to me poison?
This world is like that, sometimes to me and sometimes to you

4. To read the story of grief on the tablet of my face
The nights keep a candle burning till morn, alas, for you

5. If he does not make the stars of his tears a guide for him
In the night of grief, the lost lover can never find his way to you

6. We know, oh my heart, that you are not coming to the gathering
Just come anyway and see why and where that moon rises for you

7. O my lord, make abundant the things your servants need
For every heart's desire is eternally possible to you

8. O Necâtî, like the sun, let him turn stone into ruby
If the shah should cast a favorable gaze on you (Necâtî 1963, *gazel* no. 2; translation my own)

The poem by Mihrî:

1. I've come, rubbing my face in the dirt, making my way right to you
Oh monarch, I wish I might reveal my sorry plight to you

2. Of all the world's kings you are the king so famed for justice
That the sun comes to your door each day in service to you

3. O you rose-cheek, the nightingale of the soul recites
Praises day and night, at dawn and dusk to you

4. O my lord, the fire of jealousy has consumed this
thirsty heart in flames
Don't leave me in the darkness of grief, let Hızır be a
companion to you

5. O Mihrî, let it make you as youthful as Züleyhâ
Should the monarch turn his Yusuf-like gaze to you

It is evident that these are parallel poems because they share the same rhyme meter and refrain word: *sana*, or "to you." As Necâtî supposedly said, matching the rhyme and meter of a poem will not make the new one as worthy. However, a closer look at these two poems provides strong evidence that Mihrî was aware of the deeper meanings of Necâtî's poem and further built upon those meanings. Although these two poems are written in the *gazel* genre, they can be considered mini-*kasîdes* because of their function and structure. The function is to praise the sultan and draw his attention. Although we do not know her motivation, Mihrî followed this theme in her own poem. The structure of the two poems follows the model of the *kasîde* genre. They open with a *medh*, or praise, in the first two couplets. In the third and fourth couplets of Necâtî's poem and in the third couplet of Mihrî's poem, the poet enters the scene. The last couplets of each poem refer to two powerful, legendary men: Alexander the Great and the prophet Yusuf (according to religious texts, the most beautiful men). Mihrî follows Necâtî's poetic structure closely, having a counter line for each of Necâtî's thematic couplets, but she uses these themes in a different manner. It is in these parallels that she competes with Necâtî and illuminates the differences between herself and him. Thus, this is another place where a poet could reveal his or her poetic voice.

The poet is the main actor—the speaker—as he/she generates the love, praises the beloved with hyperbolic imagery, and communicates the impossibility of union. In Necâtî's case, according to the *tezkires*, the beloved is most likely to be the sultan. The poet's yearning for a chat, or even a glimpse, has a metaphoric meaning. When the beloved sultan looks at the poet, he recognizes the poet's talents and blesses him with his patronage—the major intention of Necâtî's poem. The layers of meaning must work not only to illuminate the surface intention, the classical yearning for union, but also the deeper intention, asking for royal attention and patronage.

From the second couplet onward, Necâtî paints a picture of an evening gathering where lovers meet, drink, and chat until dawn. He calls on the beloved for *sohbet*, or conversation, which can be understood as intimate chatting. The temporal setting of the poem is nighttime, when the moon is present, in a place where a group of people are drinking, mourning, and crying for the beloved. In the last couplet, he refers to the beloved as the sun, with its warmth and light that will illuminate everything on earth. Necâtî uses the traditionally understood relationship between the ruby and the sun to underscore his deeper meaning: calling for the sultan's attention. At the time, the ruby was believed to be a white stone. When washed with the blood of the liver and left under the sun, its color changes and it becomes red and, thus, more valuable. The blood of the liver is shed during the suffering and grieving of love. Necâtî compares himself to a ruby, asking for a gaze from the sun, which represents the sultan or the beloved. When the sultan looks at him, he is transformed into a valuable stone. In real life, when the sultan recognizes him through an appreciation of his poetry, he becomes one of the luckiest poets.

In Mihrî's case, she again focuses on praising the sultan, yet she goes even a step further, placing the beloved higher than the sun in terms of his justice—the major quality of a leader. The sun is considered just, as it spreads its light onto the world and all of its creatures each day. Still, for Mihrî, the beloved's justice exceeds that of the sun; the sun comes to the beloved's threshold and serves him.

As the imagery of the sun develops toward the last couplet, a connection between the sun and classical characters appears. For Necâtî, the beloved is the sultan compared to the sun. For Mihrî, the beloved is Yusuf. In this way, she is able to turn the use of imagery to her advantage, bringing another related character into the picture. This character, Züleyhâ, is Yusuf's female counterpart, and she is significant in Mihrî's poem because Mihrî identifies herself with Züleyhâ. The story of Yusuf and Züleyhâ is one of the classical motifs of Ottoman literature, based on the Qur'anic verse entitled "Yusuf" or the "Story of Joseph" from the Old Testament. The basic plot of the story in the Qur'an and the Bible is similar, but it is narrated in different ways. For instance, the Qur'anic version is in verse and provides few details. Unlike the biblical version, in the Qur'an, the characters know from the very beginning that Yusuf is a prophet. Based on the Qur'an, the summary of the story is as follows.

One night, Yusuf, the dearest son of Yakub, has a dream. In his vision, he sees eleven stars, the moon, and the sun bowing in front of him. He narrates his dream to his father. Yakub, being a prophet himself, understands the meaning of the dream: that his son is among the chosen ones. He asks Yusuf not to share his dream with his brothers, as he knows that his other sons are already jealous of Yusuf and, if they were to learn about his dream, they might harm him. However, Yakub cannot stop Yusuf's misfortunes. One day, his eleven brothers, tired of Yusuf being their father's favorite, decide to get rid of him. They throw him into a well, leaving him there to die, and tell their father that a wolf killed Yusuf. They show Yakub

Yusuf's shirt, stained with blood as evidence, although they had actually stained Yusuf's shirt with the blood of a wolf that they killed on the way home. Yakub is devastated, but he trusts God's willing. After some time, gypsies save him from the well and sell him to a man called "the Aziz," a title that meant "a powerful man" in Arabic. The Aziz and his wife love Yusuf, as he is a beautiful and good boy. As the years pass, the Aziz's wife falls in love with Yusuf and she attempts to seduce him. Yusuf resists the temptation, making the wife furious. In the Qur'anic version, she invites the women of the town to witness his beauty. Evidently, the women cut their hands when they see him because his beauty makes them metaphorically blind. The Aziz's wife continues trying to persuade Yusuf to be her lover. One day, while Yusuf is trying to escape her, she grabs his shirt, which tears apart in her hands. She lies to her husband and accuses Yusuf of seducing her. However, when they look at the shirt and find that it was torn from behind, they realize the truth of the matter. Nevertheless, Yusuf still wants to go to jail to escape temptation. He spends many years in jail and is only released because he can interpret the pharaoh's dream. By doing so, he helps the pharaoh survive a dreadful drought and, in return, the pharaoh appoints Yusuf as his administrator. Meanwhile, as a result of famine in Canaan, Yusuf's brothers come to Egypt to find food. Although Yusuf recognizes them at once, his brothers remain clueless that the man in front of them is their brother. After some tricks, Yusuf manages to bring his long-suffering father to Egypt. The story ends with the reunion of father and son.

A major similarity between the Qur'anic and biblical versions of the story is that neither mentions the name of Aziz's wife. However, this story was retold many times in Arabic, Persian, and Ottoman literature, transforming it into a love story between Yusuf and the wife of the Egyptian. One of the main additions to the literary versions is that the woman gains a name, Züleyhâ. Jâmî's (1414–92) literary version of the story was the most widely read and beloved in Ottoman circles. In fact, Hamdullah Hamdî (1449–1508) translated it from Persian into Turkish in the fifteenth century. We can assume, then, that Necâtî and Mihrî read Hamdî's version. In Hamdî's envisioning of the story, Züleyhâ is both the main character and the active lover who pursues her beloved, Yusuf. In contrast to the story in religious texts, which focuses on the tale of a man becoming a prophet, in the literary versions, it is Züleyhâ who undertakes the journey of transformation. Details, such as her ability to see the future in her dreams, suggest that she is no ordinary person. In the literary stories, Züleyhâ first sees Yusuf in a dream and falls in love with him. When the Aziz asks for her hand, thinking that he is Yusuf, she immediately accepts. Realizing her mistake, she suffers and never consummates her marriage with the Aziz. One day, she finally sees Yusuf in real life and she is ready to do anything that is required to win his love. For her love of him, she ignores social pressures, gives up everything she has, and leaves her husband, becoming a poor, wretched, and old woman. In this hyperbolic literary tradition, her endless weeping causes her to become old and blind. When Yusuf finds her again, he looks at her with love and compassion, and she regains her vision, youth, and beauty. After years of suffering, as both Yusuf and Züleyhâ fulfill each of their journeys, they marry and have many children.

Considering Mihrî's *telmîh* (allusion) to the story of Yusuf and Züleyhâ, it is clear that she refers to either Jâmî's version or Hamdî's retelling. Jâmî's story, as with the Sufi reinterpretation of the Qur'anic story, is an allegory of the soul's pursuit of love. In this transformed narrative, Züleyhâ is the lover obsessed with her desire for her beloved, Yusuf, the symbol of divine beauty. As the lover in the story, Züleyhâ is also the active character on whom the narrative concentrates, following her from childhood. In Jâmî and Hamdî's versions, there are many additions to the Qur'anic story, such as Züleyhâ's dreams, as well as omissions, such as details about Yusuf's family. The Qur'anic or biblical stories are about Yusuf, his relationship to other men (e.g., his father and brothers), and his path to becoming a prophet. The mystical/literary versions focus on Züleyhâ as a lover.

Mihrî's use of this story follows the literary versions. As a poet and lover, she identifies herself with Züleyhâ. She connects the mystical interpretation of the story to the overall theme of the poem, asking for a gaze and attention, just as Züleyhâ asked for the attention of Yusuf. In Mihrî's case, as she suggests in her last couplet, when the beloved casts his gaze on her, she becomes young again just like Züleyhâ.

Mihrî's choice of Züleyhâ as a character with whom to identify herself as a poet and lover is a critical part of her efforts to cast her distinctiveness as a woman poet. Although she also referred to other classical women characters in her poetry, such as Leylâ or Şirîn, she only identified herself with Züleyhâ. Like Necâtî, she used these other characters to make comparisons based on the essential meaning of the characters' names, such as a long night or sweet lips. I think that she chose to identify herself with Züleyhâ for two major reasons: first, both Züleyhâ and Mihrî were outcasts in the sense that they crossed gender and social boundaries to achieve their desires. Second, like Züleyhâ, a poet suffers to reach his/her beloved. Both women transcended gender limitations, taking on a male role as active lovers. Mihrî's self-representation through a strong female classical character provides an antecedent for her existence within the field of poetry. We may not know if Mihrî wrote this poem to get the attention of a patron in the same fashion as Necâtî, but we can see that she was capable of carefully following Necâtî's example while making fundamental changes in her parallel poem, inserting a woman's perspective as a way to highlight the distinctiveness of her voice. The comparative case of these poems by Necâtî and Mihrî demonstrates that, although Ottoman poetry has been traditionally accepted as formulaic, with no room for personal expression, it is possible to note nuances by asking relevant questions.

All of these mythical female characters—Leylâ, Şirîn, and Züleyhâ—are available in the poetic tradition as literary tools. When Mihrî portrayed herself as the embodiment of one of those classical female characters, she was still within the boundaries of tradition. Thus, she was accepted and celebrated. She simply found a space for women in the literature and used it for her purposes. She intentionally selected an active female character from the stock images to represent herself as a distinct, but still valid, member of the poetic world. Thus we can conclude that Züleyhâ served Mihrî's purposes of representing herself well.

Claims of manliness and a subversive self-representation, however, would not have sufficed to secure Mihrî a place as a poet on the battlefield of poetry. She also needed to resist her colleagues who wanted to represent her as a beloved. In the poetic dialogue between Mihrî and Makâmî that is discussed in the next chapter, she demonstrates her insistence on being an active lover or a poet, as opposed to the silent role of the beloved. In her dialogues with Makâmî, she applies another strategy to avoid her colleague's romantic advances with the help of a traditional tool: humor. As with her use of mythical characters, she demonstrated that the poetic tradition could be used for her subversive purposes. In both cases, she naturally challenged the conventions by taking the role of the male speaker and generating a rupture.

6

Gender-Bending and Subversion

Makâmî and Mihrî

The poetic dialogues between Mihrî and her male colleagues demonstrate that she did not shy away from battling with her male colleagues through poetry; rather, she took them as opportunities to prove herself as a poet. In these dialogues, particularly those with Makâmî, she showed that she could be courageous on the battlefield of poetry and that she could use the traditional aesthetic tools to her advantage. As these dialogues were eventually recorded in writing and survived in a literary history, we can make an educated guess and assume that they occurred in *meclises* hosted and attended by the elite circles of the time.

These dialogues are significant evidence of the performative nature of the poetic tradition and its aesthetics. A comparative analysis of such poems shows that there are a series of acts and rhetorical language used to compose poetry and to make the claim of being a poet. Identifying Mihrî's strategies not only highlights her legitimation process as a poet, but also explains the acceptance of her subversiveness. Poets, whether men or women, establish their mastery in the field through a series of performative acts. Mihrî follows this same route, but also masterfully manipulates it so that her difference is accepted. Thus, her legitimation and subversion work together and at the same time.

In addition, her dialogue with Makâmî demonstrates her insistence on being an active lover or a poet, as opposed to the submissive role of a beloved. She shows how, in a woman's voice, traditional tools such as humor can be ironic but also subversive.

Humor as a Dismantling Tool

Ottomans took humor seriously. Although modern scholarship has considered humorous texts a part of folk literature—and, by implication, less important—the founders and first critics of classical literature (i.e., the writers of the first biographical dictionaries) defined, categorized, and evaluated different kinds of humor. Among the terminology used to define humor in the *tezkires* are *hiciv*, *hezl*, *tarîz*, and *şathiyye* for satire and *nükte*, *latîfe*, *şaka*, and *suhriyye* for humor. Although *tezkire* writers do not specifically define what constitutes each category, they give examples from well-known poets. Humor aside, from their didactic stories, it is clear that these writers were cautious about satire. For instance, they tell the story of the poet Nef'î who was famous for his lampoons and ended up losing his life. Among the categories of humor, *nükte* (a clever point) seems to have been the most valued. Apparently, a poet who was adept at using *nükte* (called *nüktedân*, *nüktedâr*, *nükteâmîz*, *nükteşinâs*, *nüktegû*, or *nüktepîrâ*) was rare and therefore highly valued. The reason it was difficult to construct a *nükte*, according to Mine Mengi (2010, 31), was related to its close relationship with *mana* (conceit) or *mazmun* (witticism). A good poem had to be ambiguous in a way that forced the target audience to recognize and appreciate the correct but not necessarily the most obvious meaning. All of these literary tools were intended to make the meaning compact and deeper.

Apart from the humorous poems, there was a specific genre called *letâifnâme* (the pleasantries). From the sixteenth century onward, while *tezkires* were creating literary history by anthologizing, *letâifnâmes* were compiling jokes and became very popular. In his introduction to his *letâifnâme*, Lâmiizâde lists the benefits of humor, intellectual development being one of them. Likewise, in his humorous but also sexually explicit text, *Dâfi'ü'l-gumûm ve râfi'ü'l-humûm* (Repeller of Sorrows and Removers of Worry), the sixteenth-century poet al-Gazalî suggests that his work is intended to be educational (Kuru 2000). As *tezkire* writers show, the combination of humor and eroticism challenges social norms while remaining entertainment. By employing a grotesque language, they reveal an intimate circle in which members laugh at one another and make fun of not only social norms but also the highly stylized poetic tradition.

In the following discussion, I intend to show the alternative ways in which humor could be used by a male and a female poet. Whereas Makâmî's use of humor enforces gender roles, in Mihrî's hands it helps her to subvert those very norms.

Poet versus Beloved: Makâmî and Mihrî

Among the poets with whom Mihrî entered a poetic dialogue, only that between her and Makâmî, another regular at Şehzâde Ahmed's court, is recorded in literary history. Although she did not refrain from mentioning male names as beloveds (e.g., İskender) or colleagues (e.g., Müeyyedzâde or Necâtî) in her poetry, for the most part, her male colleagues' responses, if there were any, were not recorded in written history. Makâmî not only engaged in a poetic dialogue with her, but he clearly pronounced her name in his poems. Although these poems did not survive in a collection, parts of them appear in the *tezkires* and in one of Mihrî's divans.

As Âşık reports in his entry for Makâmî, he was an imam in Amasya during Şehzâde Ahmed's tenure. Although we do not know his real name or background information, he was a musician as well as a poet who composed under the *mahlas* of Makâmî (meaning belonging to a musical mode). He also worked as a teacher in the prince's palace, teaching the boys Qur'an and music. In his entry for Makâmî, Âşık briefly mentions his beautiful musical compositions and his poetic dialogue with Mihrî. Besides the poetic dialogue, which I will discuss in detail later, the following lines are an example of his poetry, extracted from his *kasîde* for Mihrî, which appears in her divan.[1] The tone of the poem is erotically humorous and identifies Mihrî as a beloved. He directly addresses her, reminding her of his unrequited love:

> No wonder he gave up the ghost in your neighborhood
> If it is your servant Makâmî's fate to go to heaven
>
> Truly your lip was once the water of life [to him]
> You didn't grant it to that ailing one and he died.
>
> Truly you were once at the top of the list of beauties
> Now your time has passed, Oh idol, go and toss it in the water.
>
> Makâmî passed in exile and you never once said to him
> Come here and wait at my threshold with my dogs

In this poem, Makâmî presents himself as a lover and Mihrî as a beloved. According to him, she has many lovers and he wants to be one of them, but she does not accept him. He says that he is lovesick and could be cured by her kiss. As expected from a beloved, she is cruel and will not cure him or return his love. Makâmî uses the past tense to relate that this occurred a long

1. The poem, entitled "Mesnevi-i Latîf," is found in Mihrî Hâtun Dîvanı, 3974 Ayasofya, Süleymaniye Library, Istanbul.

time ago, when he had told her to enjoy her youth and beauty. However, he could not convince her:

> When your peaches were ripe in the orchard of beauty
> Didn't I say to you, don't hide them, sell them in time.

Because she did not listen to his advice, she died before enjoying the blessing of love. He closes the poem with a reference to her grave:

> If you should pass by her grave, you should hear
> The green plants there calling out, "Mihrî, Mihrî"

Because Makâmî talks about her in the past tense, it is likely that he composed this poem after her death to commemorate his friend. Her passing before him might suggest that Makâmî was younger than Mihrî. Similarly, in the poetic dialogue that follows between them, Mihrî insinuates that her body is dysfunctional, which might suggest old age. The age gap and her references to her decaying body might be the reason for their carelessness toward writing poetry to one another and explicitly mentioning one another's names. The *tezkire* writers did not suggest a love affair between them, despite their tendency to suggest romantic possibilities between Mihrî and any number of men. Makâmî and Mihrî seem to have been comfortable enough with one another to joke about sensitive issues such as love between a man and a woman. Regardless of the reasons, the poetic dialogue between them is fundamentally different than the one between her and Necâtî. Because the dialogue was reciprocal, it implies a real-life encounter in a social setting, such as a *meclis.* They go beyond a textual communication and reflect a performance involving an audience. Apart from an equally balanced dialogue between the two speakers, the poems represent an intimacy that can grow among the fellow poets of a certain *meclis.* This intimate language is pronounced in their use of the discourse of love and, in particular, Mihrî's use of an erotically humorous tone.

Regardless of the background, their poems present an opportunity to discuss the performativity of the poetic discourse and how it can function differently in different situations. Moreover, they show the versatility of the discourse in different poets' works. While Mihrî's parallel poems to Necâtî legitimized her poetic skills and allowed her to demonstrate her exceptionality in a larger context, beyond the limits of her *meclis*, her responses to Makâmî show how she could manipulate the poetic discourse to her advantage and, furthermore, that this would be acceptable among a close circle of friends. Because Makâmî puts her in the category of the beloved in his poem, she makes use of humor, a traditional tool, to denounce the situation. Her use of humor is fundamentally different than that of Zâtî, as mentioned in chapter 1. Whereas in Zâtî's poem humor enforces traditional gender roles, in Mihrî's poem it helps to challenge them.

My discussion of Mihrî in intellectual history shows how humor, along with eroticism, assisted in conceptualizing morally loaded issues, such as women and gender, in a playful and lighthearted way. As I have discussed before, *tezkire* writers' erotically humorous discourse triggers a Bakhtinian carnivalesque laughter in the audience, which temporarily causes a short-term awareness and allows a critical glimpse of the structure of the poetic language and its conceptualization of gender. As it is only for a limited amount of time, it does not threaten to change or deconstruct this structure. For this reason, it is one of the ways in which the limits of the dominant poetic discourse can be stretched. Besides its provocative function, humor can also be useful for poets who try to create complex and profound meanings. As they compete with one another to create original meanings from a limited rhetorical language, literary tools, such as allusion and hyperbole, play significant roles. Their intention is to construct layers of meaning with the least amount of word economy (*teksîf*), a literary art in and of itself. Therefore, humor and eroticism can be useful for attracting attention to certain issues, as well as in helping poets achieve their intention of building layered meanings.

My reading of humor in conjunction with eroticism pays deliberate attention to its take on gender and sexuality. Based on a Bakhtinian approach, I evaluate the use of humor as a legitimate tool to criticize social norms. In the following humorous dialogue between Makâmî and Mihrî, we see how she embedded her criticism of the poetic discourse and by implication its dismissal of women, in her response. Makâmî's poem, as quoted by Âşık, must have been written first:

> Your beauty is the sun, and the new moon
> What bends the crescent moon is pain for your eyebrows
>
> The peacock tail drew on the tablet of your beauty
> As if your curl were the Royal Signatory on your beauty's
> warrant
>
> The peach-fuzz on your face, the mole on your cheek the
> curl and lashes
> Each one of them is black painful pang to the sick at heart
> My pledge is this, that I will give my life in exchange for a
> kiss
> Proffer your lips and don't suppose that Makâmî is a liar
> (Âşık Çelebi 2010, 826–27; translation my own)

Makâmî's poem echoes the *tezkire* writers' assertion that Mihrî was so beautiful and talented that many people, including Makâmî himself, showed interest, although she refused them all. Even though she did not reciprocate his affections, she entered into a poetic dialogue with Makâmî. In a poem that appears in her divan, she seems to respond to the above lines. In a joking voice, Mihrî discusses the issue of Makâmî's affection for her:

My beauty is neither the sun nor is it the new moon
Neither are my eyebrows bows, nor my curl a Royal
  Signatory

The preacher accused us falsely, calling us beautiful
The number one poets are the biggest liars

It is no surprise if he asks us for a kiss in jest
Anyone whose beard grows in becomes the people's
  laughing stock

From now on Makâmî, our only kisses will be
Years of angina and the torment of diarrhea[2]

In Makâmî's poem, his infatuation with Mihrî's beauty is clear. He makes a connection between her and her name, using the meaning of her name, "pertaining to the sun," to compare her beauty to that of the sun. Although we do not know Makâmî's intentions, in this poem, he takes the role of the poet/lover, giving the role of the beloved to Mihrî. The silent and sexualized role of the beloved, however, is undesirable for Mihrî as a woman poet. She refuses his compliments and, using a literary tool, *nükte*, she begins a rhetorical game with him. She calls him a preacher and implies that his words should not be taken seriously. Besides the reference to his job as an imam, Mihrî's reasoning is that a poet is a performer and his words are only rhetorical. In this game, as she suggests, many poets are liars. Far from reflecting their true feelings,

2. See appendix, poem no. 6.

they only follow a tradition. Since Makâmî is a poet, his assertions about Mihrî must be lies as well.

While resisting the role of the beloved and the classical associations with this role, such as silence and timidity, Mihrî highlights the performative aspect of poetry and her own satirical take on it. She shows how it can be only rhetorical, if not pretentious, role play. As a continuation of Makâmî's couplet, she mocks his intentions as a lover and her potential as a beloved. Mihrî is far from upset with Makâmî; instead, she says she is unsurprised by him asking for a kiss. She makes fun of him as he begs for a kiss, telling him that the only kisses he will get from her is angina and pain of diarrhea. This may be a reference to her old age. As the language turns to the grotesque, the erotic aura is replaced with mundane reality. The absurdity of the two juxtaposed worlds, the romantic and worldly, generates surprise and, eventually, a Bakhtinian carnivalesque laughter. Her references to bodily dysfunctions may seem out of place, but they evoke a laughter that sheds momentary light on the pretentious rhetoric of the poetic discourse. In this way, she not only criticizes the abstraction of the lover and the beloved within the dominant discourse, but also asserts herself as an active poet rather than a passive beloved. The comparison of Makâmî and Mihrî's perspective on the discourse of love shows that they both compose with the same traditional tools, but that their take on it is quite different. Whereas Makâmî's poem remains within the traditional norm, Mihrî's parody is subversive. Instead of being upset with Makâmî, she playfully takes a sober position, mocking his traditional voice.

Mihrî responds to Makâmî in erotically humorous discourse, which was pervasive in the early modern poetic world. For instance, Zâtî's poem, as quoted in the *tezkires* and discussed in chapter 1 of this book, is a good example of the ways in which poets discussed gendered issues. Zâtî's grotesque language highlights the absurdity of Paşa Çelebi asking for Mihrî's hand. The difference between his and Mihrî's use of the same discourse, however, can be seen in her response to Makâmî. Whereas the male poet's humor enforces gender roles, her appropriation challenges the norms. Once again, she implies the performative construction of poetic love and its pretentious, symbolic acts. Mihrî was aware of the poetic tradition's aesthetic and social limitations for women and was not reluctant to criticize it. As such, humor works in her poetry as an agent to provoke a rupture in the conventions.

❀

Mihrî's process of becoming a woman poet shows that poetry is performative and it involves certain manners and rhetoric that were constructed with the assumption that both the speaker and the audience were men (masculine/active or feminine/passive). Mihrî's process also shows that this poetic discourse can be manipulated. The difficulty for a woman becoming an active player in the literary scene or playing the role of the lover/poet lay in the fact that these roles were traditionally reserved for men. The woman poet must confront the centuries-old claim of manliness as the basis of poethood. Thus, Mihrî worked to challenge the definition of manliness as a male quality so that she, as a woman, might be included.

Conversely, the aesthetic ideal of a rhetorical love between the male poet and the male beloved was complicated by the entrance of a woman poet, as her poems imply a courtship between a woman poet and male beloved. In the traditional structure of love, women represented worldliness, in opposition to the spiritual male world that was represented in poetry. In this vein, it is no wonder that Mihrî claims manliness as a poet or identifies herself with Züleyhâ, one of the few classical female characters in the poetic tradition to take an active role in spiritual love. A claim without proof has no value, though. Thus, she worked to prove her point by entering the battlefield of poetry, writing *nazîres* to respected poets to show that her poetry was as good as theirs and that she was worthy of entering the competition. Because her strategies were legitimate, she not only was accepted but transcended the meaning of poethood.

Mihrî's work is an early example of Ottoman women's writing, and it shows a systematic divergence from the dominant poetic discourse. From this close analysis of Mihrî's poetry, it is apparent that her writing was legitimately distinct from that discourse. Although legitimacy and distinctiveness may seem to be antithetical, they were relatively consecutive steps of her writing process.

As discussed in the previous chapters, a poet needed to build networks through his or her poetry. One of the major motivations was to attract a patron. A celebrity poet, such as Necâtî, also needed a patron and composed poetry to reach this goal. Like the roles of lover and beloved, poet and patron are also historical processes. Later in his life, Necâtî became a patron of poets himself. Composing poetry for colleagues was another way to legitimate one's own poetry and to challenge one's peers. Mihrî followed these steps to carve out a space in the poetic world for herself. However, a woman poet had to make smart decisions to be approved by the community of poets. She needed to be careful about choosing a patron and competing with fellow poets on equal terms.

Mihrî's acceptance by this community was a milestone in her career. Her awareness of this milestone is a sign of her distinctiveness as a poet. Although she was accepted, because of her limited opportunities she would never hold an administrative position at the palace, as Necâtî or women poets of later periods such as Ayşe Hubbî did. Even though her poetic skills were comparable to that of Necâtî, because of the marginal position of her gender, she was forced to constantly prove herself to her peers. Consequently, her critique of the traditions—such as the manliness of a poet or the rhetorical nature of love—is evident in her poetry. Although the tradition trapped her in a permanent marginal position, she eventually used this as a tool to carve herself a distinct place in intellectual history.

Epilogue

Returning to the Future

For the people of the time being a Turk is an honor
Would that I were garlic in their sour tarhana soup[1]

In this book I tried to explain the making of Mihrî Hatun based on her circumstances and her subversive voice in the intellectual discourse. As I discussed in detail in the previous pages, her existence in the early modern Ottoman times was both legitimate and challenging to the social norms at large. Although it focused on Mihrî's writing, the discussion showed how, to grasp her story, it was necessary to look simultaneously into her privileged and intellectual world. The idea of the woman poet in the backdrop made it possible to show how she perceived herself as an active participant in the intellectual world of her time.

The epigraph is yet another example of Mihrî's writing: first, a construction of layers of meanings that was not only considered a good performance but also an outlet to insert her ideas; and second, a subversive use of rhetorical language. In these specific lines, she writes that people of her time

1. See appendix, poem no. 17.

considered being a Turk (*Türklük*) as a source of pride. In light of this, she adds, she wishes to be garlic in their *tarhana* soup.[2] At first the two lines do not make sense together. However, a closer look will reveal a smart reversal in her narrative and a sarcastic tone that makes fun of the state of the field and her place in it as a woman poet.

As mentioned primarily in part 1, Mihrî wrote in a time when Ottoman poetry was becoming a tradition of its own, and this was reiterated in the *tezkires*. It was a time when urban entertainment centers were emerging and, as a consequence of centralization, poetry was institutionalized and historicized. One of the urban centers of this early modern period was her beloved hometown, Amasya, which had been a hub for the arts and sciences not only for Turks, but also for immigrants like the Persians. With the parallel process of urbanization/centralization and the evolution of the classical tradition in the emerging compilations of histories (e.g., *tezkires*), Ottoman intellectual field was becoming a tradition of its own. As Ottoman arts and literature was developing into a tradition, the cultivation of a lifestyle in and around the urban centers, as opposed to the simplicity of the countryside, became pronounced. One of the outcomes of this turning point in Ottoman literary history, as suggested in this book, is the welcoming of the woman poet.

Mihrî's lines in the epigraph suggest that being Turkish—as opposed to being Persian, a culture that had influenced the Ottoman poetry or, better yet, being a Rûmî, which was

2. I appreciate Mary Işın's feedback after reading my article (Havlioğlu 2010a), which discusses this poem briefly. Işın suggested that, according to historical documents such as Evliyâ Çelebi (2003, 5, 27), the *tarhana* soup can be prepared in various ways in different areas of Anatolia.

preferred among the intellectual circles[3]—is now considered honorable. In classical poetry, such as in the great Persian poet Hafez's use of the "Shirazi Turk," the term "Turk" meant both beautiful and cruel as the beloved should be.[4] As Kafadar (2007) suggests, "a good intellectual or artist may have boasted that the Rûmis had outdone the Acems or Arabs," but a Turk does not represent the honorable or sophisticated lifestyle. Mihrî communicates the absurd situation by mentioning their simple eating habits, such as their traditional soup, *tarhana*. *Tarhana* is prepared in almost all parts of Anatolia. It is the basic food for all, particularly for the peasants and the working class. She makes the connection between the soup and being a Turk with a clever move that reveals her skills in poetry. In eastern parts of Anatolia, garlic or other kinds of herbs are occasionally added to *tarhana* as an extra flavor. She uses the common word *sûm* for garlic, but also evokes an idiom, *Türk-i Rûstâyân* (literally, the Turk of the village), which also meant garlic. In this way, she makes an implicit connection (*tenâsüb*) between Turk and garlic. She is playfully making a statement: if the taste of the audience is changing, I will be their extra flavor. Comparing herself to garlic might seem odd, but, by now, the witticism of Mihrî's voice is familiar to us. She uses this tone to draw attention to the situation, the change of standards poetry, and her place as a woman—the new actor in the rhetorical game.

❀

Analysis of Mihrî Hatun's writing can affect the ways in which women have been contextualized within Ottoman/Turkish

3. For a detailed discussion of the terms "Turk" and "Rûmî," see Kafadar 2007.

4. Franklin Lewis (1995, 22) discusses Hafez's use of "Turk."

intellectual history. In this book, I have attempted to explain the possible reasons behind Mihrî's success and survival in early modern Ottoman intellectual circles within the frameworks of the sociological and literary agendas of her time. In a period in which there was almost no record of women as producers of culture, the making of Mihrî Hatun shows the literary tradition from an unprecedented perspective. Her circumstances, such as her background, in addition to her networks from an influential province, suggest how her privileged life could help a woman to become a legitimate poet. Although her social and economic background could have been helpful for an aspiring woman poet such as Mihrî, her successful reception as a woman in the literary circles of her time, as well as in the centuries that followed, were due to her mastery of literary composition.

Since biographers first chronicled her life story and evaluated her work, Mihrî Hatun has been well known. Due to the uncritical attempts at explaining her existence and acceptance in literary history, she was not considered part of the history of women's writing in Turkish. This book has tried to show that Mihrî Hatun's writing not only reflects what it means to be a woman at her time but also highlights her consistent strategies to exist and endure in an intellectual tradition that does not necessarily include women. Women's representation in the first literary histories (i.e., the *tezkires*) is only the starting point of a critical approach to women in intellectual history. It provides a ground to situate a woman's voice as she speaks for and against an existing intellectual discourse. As I tried to show, her marginal position, which is clear in the *tezkires*, can be to her advantage to insert herself as a distinct new member of the literary circles.

Presumably, one of the primary questions this book will evoke relates to the choice I have made to discuss "women" as a separate gender category in the early modern period. The strategic essentialism this book adopts is based on the way a woman poet was perceived in historical documents and in Mihrî's own writing. As I have tried to explain previously, Mihrî was first a woman and then a poet in literary history. Consequently, her position as a poet in the aesthetic discourse of love ignores her gender as a speaker, which she had to adopt and transform at the same time. Nevertheless, it is also my intention to go beyond this prescribed positioning by trying to understand the meaning of "woman" within the gender matrix of the early modern Ottoman literary discourse.

The comparisons between Mihrî and Necâtî or Makâmî show not only her given positioning as a woman within the literary tradition, but also the necessary emergence of her dissent. The comparative cases also highlight the performativity of poetry as a historical and social process, which can function in different ways in accordance with the poet's intentions. In this frame, my approach is based on concepts of subject position, marginality, and performativity to contextualize Mihrî's poetic voice in its historical, social, and literary background.

From the perspective of performance, it is clear that in almost all of her poems, Mihrî purposefully represents her poetic voice as a marginal force that persuasively insinuates a reconsideration of the norms. Through these two aspects of her composition, she simultaneously legitimizes her place in the poetic world and subverts the very tradition that she uses in her poetry. Moreover, considering Mihrî within the larger picture of intellectual history, she is not marginal but rather the first known example of women's writing.

Through such an approach, we learn from Mihrî's story and her poetry that, while poetry was a male gendered space in both a physical and aesthetic sense, a woman could be a legitimate and celebrated poet in the late fifteenth and early sixteenth centuries. Mihrî's existence and success has three main implications: first, she could be part of the *meclis* culture because it was the space where poetry was produced and recorded in *tezkires*. However, the *tezkires* do not address this question, as if this was not an issue for them. Though Ottomans practiced gender segregation, Mihrî and other women poets' existence in male literary history prove that, when it comes to the intimate space of artistic production in early modern Ottoman times, our knowledge is very limited. Apart from the existence of women poets, the poetry displays a dichotomy between the poetic and the mundane worlds. It seems very likely that the code of conduct in the literary circles was quite different from that of other social groups. The *meclis* culture is not consistent throughout history and its spatial dimensions might show difference from one place to another. Mihrî's story demonstrates how Amasya and Bayezid were important components of the intellectual circles of her time.

The second implication of Mihrî's existence and success is that a woman could have the necessary education to perform poetry and compose love poems. Thanks to the master/apprentice tradition, as opposed to institutionalized education, a woman could receive the education necessary to become a poet. Mihrî and Müeyyedzâde are significant examples because they represent an intimate professional relationship that was instrumental in her intellectual endeavors. Her relationships with Müeyyedzâde and other male poets illustrate how a man and a woman could engage in intellectual pursuits together.

Finally, because she was able to become a poet without having to disguise her gender identity, Mihrî challenges the understanding of poetry as being a male-dominated space. After her poems, it is no longer possible to treat poetry as only a male business. Furthermore, her success and acceptance ultimately point to a shift in gender construction in poetry. She evidently was marginal, as is clear from the overwhelming numbers of male poets in comparison to the few women in the field and the homosocial discourse of love. Within the spatial and discursive boundaries, a woman is de facto marginal based on her biology and the values attached to her gender. As the *tezkire* writers show, however, the woman poet was the desirable new actor at a time when Ottoman poetry was becoming a tradition of its own. While narrating the first history of Ottoman literature, the male critics' discourse reveals the marginal position of a woman vis-à-vis the literary tradition and how entries for women poets such as Mihrî were the catalysts to showing the gender construction in poetry. As a woman, she both reinforces and challenges the manly qualities of the poetic discourse.

Although the *tezkire* writers included a well-selected list of women poets, they took the opportunity to reconstruct gender ambiguity for women as a value in poetic discourse. Although both the lover/poet and the beloved are male, they interchangeably play the active/controlling/dominant role or the passive/submissive role. In terms of initiating love, the lover seems to be dominant and manly on the surface. In fact, the beloved, in his absolute silence, is the one who controls the lover's desire and torments him/her by not paying attention. Both roles are prescribed for a male actor with varying qualities that could be categorized as masculine or feminine today. However, because these qualities are not fixed but attributed only to the male gender, the categories are blurry. By adopting an elusive discourse, which I call erotically humorous, *tezkire* writers represented the blurry borders between the genders in the poetic landscape. Until Mihrî, only men could be the lovers. Based on her skills in poetry, the woman poet complicates this structure in such a way that, just like the lover or the beloved, she can be an androgynous actor in the love narrative. By taking the male role of the poet as a woman, she represents herself as a "manly" woman. It is for this reason, I argue, that she is not only accepted, but also celebrated.

The *tezkire* writers' playful use of gendered vocabulary and intentional mix and match of gendered words have an erotic and humorous effect. Eroticism and humor help in discussing morally loaded issues in a way that does not necessarily threaten the moral system at large, but makes its borders more clearly defined for the audience. In this temporary awareness, the biographers introduce the woman poet in the traditionally male field of poetry as another androgynous actor.

If we turn to Mihrî's poetry, however, the use of erotically humorous discourse has a fundamentally different effect. While she adopts the androgynous voice, she uses it to her advantage. Though the meaning of "woman" was derogatory in the Ottoman poetic discourse, for instance, she was not apologetic about her gender. In her hands, her marginal position as a woman becomes a tool to challenge the discourse she speaks from within. By doing so, she eventually redefines its core values. First and foremost, she proves that the poet does not have to be a man. Furthermore, the values attached to poethood have nothing to do with biology, but rather with being part of a group that subscribes to a certain lifestyle. Within this group's specific value system, if a man could be submissive (either as a lover or beloved), then a woman could also be manly. The manly woman poet, in other words, is not an inappropriate addition to the poetic tradition.

Apart from her marginal role in poetry, Mihrî's existence in the gender equation brings another variable into focus: age. Based on the relatively recent literature, such as Leslie Peirce and Khaled El-Rouayheb's studies, age played a significant role in early modern times. Within Mihrî's portrayal in *tezkires* and in her own poetry, it is clear that virginity and seniority—both of which imply sexual abstinence—could provide agency to women, not only among homosocial settings, but also in male spaces. In other words, virginity and seniority also imply either no sexual activity or a less defined gender identity. It is likely that some of her poems, such as her responses to Makâmî, may correspond to her later years, when she could enter a male *meclis* and engage in an erotically humorous dialogue with a male colleague while maintaining her respectability.

We also learn from Mihrî that she was careful not to cross certain lines. Though it was accepted among male poets, promiscuity and pornography do not appear in her poems. It is important to define the difference between eroticism, an integral part of poetry, and pornography, which seems to be beyond the limits for a woman. Considering their interest in gender and sexuality, *tezkire* writers carefully construct an erotic and humorous language to speak of women poets, but it rarely becomes grotesque. Besides Zâtî's curious poem about Paşa Çelebi and his supposed marriage proposal to Mihrî, which was most likely performed in an intimate male *meclis*, the stories of women poets remain within the boundaries of the erotic but still respectable. Likewise, in Mihrî's poetry, we see some necessary eroticism and humor that help to convey her meaning, but it remains within the permissible range for a respectable woman. She does not risk her reputation as a woman and, in some cases (as discussed in her dialogue with Makâmî), we see that she makes fun of flirtatious attempts by her colleagues because she finds them inappropriate. Her use of eroticism tells us what is desirable in poetry. She does play with the blurry lines of gender, like when she plays the active role of a man. When a woman poet is clear about her gender while performing the manly role of a poet, without changing anything about the beloved, she fundamentally challenges the love structure, as it is not exclusively among men anymore.

My approach in this book is based on the idea that literature reflects socioeconomic, political, and historical conditions. For this reason, I do not take literary texts at face value. Whether in the fields of literature, history, architecture, or the visual arts, texts are only meaningful in relation to each other. For instance, there is no doubt that an early modern poem has its literary meanings within its aesthetic system, but it is more complex when considered within a corpus of related texts. Along the same lines, Victoria Holbrook's (1994) use of the Kristevan concept of intertextuality in her reading of Şeyh Galib's *Hüsn ü Aşk* shows how Galib's poem has many other texts in its making, such as Rûmî's *Mesnevî* or Attar's *Conference of the Birds.* If we follow Holbrook's footsteps, Mihrî's poetic persona would not be complete if we did not consider *tezkires*, other women poets' work, and Necâtî and Makâmî's poetry alongside her own. Moreover, we would miss a great deal of information about her motivations for composing poetry if we did not consider Bayezid II, Şehzâde Ahmed, Gülbahar, and Bülbül Hatun's patronage, which can still be traced in the architectural history of the city of Amasya. The political networks at the time were significant for the composition and consumption of literature. In short, a poet's work cannot be complete without a combination of a close reading and a comparative evaluation of that work within the poet's time and place.

❀

This book intends to contribute to the growing body of research on women in the Ottoman intellectual history and Middle Eastern women's studies at large—research that has primarily focused on the nineteenth and early twentieth centuries due to lack of sources. As there has not been an inclusive attempt to contextualize women's writing before the modern period, the analyses of women's participation in intellectual history was confined to discourses of modernity or postcolonial frameworks. This book will participate in efforts to historicize women's writing in Turkish before the nineteenth century.

As Mihrî's story shows, rather than a sudden incident in the nineteenth century, women's emergence has a longer history and tradition. To show this tradition as a historical process, I suggest that nineteenth-century women writers should be compared to earlier writers. Women writers such as Fatma Aliye and their relentless reference to their predecessors or peers demonstrates that they are aware of the centuries-long tradition in which they participate.[5] As modernization favored the genre of the novel and neglected the classical tradition, women writers (particularly Fatma Aliye) were persuaded alongside the men to write prose instead of poetry. Thus, the women writers of the nineteenth century appeared to be the first women writers to compose in Turkish. The blossoming of women writers in later periods was not due to a sudden liberation of women; instead, it reflected modernization that did not always coincide with liberation. Likewise, recent studies of the modern period, such as Ayfer Karakaya-Stump's (2003) study of women's magazines during the wake of the second constitutional era (1908–9), suggest that the growth of women's writing in this period should be evaluated as part of the project of modernization and nationalization led by male intellectuals. Karakaya-Stump highlights the

5. I have previously discussed women poets acknowledging each other (see Havlioğlu 2010b).

active involvement of male intellectuals in the making of the modern Ottoman woman. In his study of more contemporary women's magazines, Irvin C. Schick (2011) suggests a direct link between the sexual agency of women and print capitalism. In other words, women's involvement in the nineteenth- and twentieth-century intellectual fields should be evaluated not only within its circumstances but also in comparison to earlier periods. From a modernist point of view, it is not surprising that classical periods and its women writers were dismissed. However, analyzing Mihrî and other early women poets in comparison to women from the nineteenth or twentieth centuries can be helpful to understand the historical process of women's writing and to contextualize these women writers in intellectual history.

To better illustrate my claim, I offer the example of Fatma Aliye (1862–1936) and the influence of her mentor, Ahmet Mithat Efendi (1844–1912). Fatma Aliye's story is comparable to that of Mihrî's: both were considered the "first" women writers of their times and representative of a paradigmatic shift in literary history. While Mihrî was the new member of the early modern literary male club, Fatma Aliye was the role model of modern Ottoman women. Evaluating Fatma Aliye's career in light of Mihrî's story will confirm that the making of women writers has a historical tradition, but that this is only a part of their making as writers. Without a deliberate analysis of their own writing, a lot of detail is missed. Although they were encouraged by the ideologies of their times, their writing was a place of both legitimation and subversion of the discourse in which they had to compose and survive.

Fatma Aliye was the daughter of historian and statesman Ahmet Cevdet Paşa. Ahmet Mithat was one of the leading intellectuals of the nineteenth century who wrote popular novels and published influential newspapers. Although Fatma

Aliye later said that she grew up reading Ahmet Mithat's novels, their first encounter occurred after she translated a book from French to Ottoman Turkish in 1890. Her translation of Georges Ohnet's *Volonté* under the title *Meram*, which she signed as "a lady," was an unprecedented success. It caused heated debates in periodicals, some of which took place on the pages of Ahmet Mithat's newspaper, *Tercüman-ı Hakikat* (Interpretation of Truth). Speculations about the identity of the translator highlighted the overall assumption that no Ottoman woman would have such a strong command of language, neither in Ottoman Turkish nor French. Ahmet Mithat wrote several articles praising the unknown woman's translation and discussing the achievements of Ottoman women, which he attributed to recent developments in the Ottoman education system during the nineteenth century. He summed up the discussion in his preface to Fatma Aliye's later novels:

> Thanks to the improvements in Ottoman education, there are indeed women who could write as well as men, and let's tame our male dignity a little bit and be honest, women who can write better than men are not rare.[6]

After this exhilarating success, Fatma Aliye wrote a letter to Ahmet Mithat expressing her gratitude for his interest in her work. She signed the letter with her recently earned title, *mütercime-i Meram*, the translator of *Meram*. This began the lifelong intellectual friendship between Ahmet Mithat and Fatma Aliye, which continued mostly through letters. A year later, they coauthored their first serialized novel, *Hayal ve Hakikat* (Dream and Reality).

6. For Ahmet Mithat's article on Fatma Aliye's achievement, see Fatma Aliye Hanım 2012, 7–8 (translation my own).

Fatma Aliye was one of the most influential figures of the nineteenth-century Ottoman intellectual world. She published novels as well as articles in periodicals about the conditions of Ottoman women. After proving herself with her translation of *Volonté*, her father began to have regular conversations with her about philosophy, history, and religion. As for her relationship with Ahmet Mithat, she was not only his foster daughter, but also his foremost student. The image of Fatma Aliye in the intellectual Ottoman world represents the collaborative project of Fatma Aliye and Ahmet Mithat to construct the modern woman author in an Ottoman context. This successful project can be seen within Mithat's biography of her, *Fatma Aliye Hanım yahud Bir Muharrire-i Osmaniye'nin Neşeti* (Fatma Aliye Hanım: An Ottoman Woman Writer Is Born). He portrays her as an extraordinary woman eager to take part in the new intellectual world. Fatma Aliye's own take on the modern woman is clearly discussed in her *Nisvân-ı Islâm* (Women of Islam), a manifesto that called for Ottoman women to take part in the modern world. A comparison of these works reveals their mutual intent to construct a model for the Ottoman woman who, according to them, should be educated in both Eastern and Western sciences, along with having strong ties to Ottoman traditions and Islam.

At first glance, we might not question the reasons behind Fatma Aliye's decision to use a pseudonym when she published *Meram*. Often, primarily in European literatures, women took male names to claim authorship or authority.[7] Fatma Aliye's initial use of a pseudonym could be seen by those studying

7. For example, Mary Shelly used her husband's name to publish *Frankenstein* in the eighteenth century. Charlotte Brontë used a male name to publish *Jane Eyre*, and some women writers continued to use male names throughout their careers, as in the case of George Eliot.

modern Turkish literature as a woman's struggle to be included in the Ottoman literary scene. However, viewing the matter from the perspective of Ottoman intellectual history, there is something peculiar about her reluctance to use her name. First, she did not try to hide her gender, only her identity. She probably did not feel the need to do so; in the Ottoman literary scene of the nineteenth century, there were several women writers who wrote for women's magazines and published volumes of their poetry. Moreover, there have been many women poets in Ottoman literary history who never felt the need to hide their gender identities. It is true that all poets, men and women, used *mahlases* (pen names), but this was for aesthetic reasons, not for hiding their identities. Fatma Aliye's use of a pseudonym might have been due to a personal reason, but it may also suggest an alternative function of the practice in the nineteenth century. When we look at women's magazines—the reflection of the growing interest in women's issues—we see that they were almost all published by men. These men contributed their own literary and opinion pieces, sometimes using female pseudonyms. As Ayfer Karakaya-Stump (2003) reports, Enis Avni signed his pieces with the name Seniha Hikmet, suggesting a pressing need for a female voice to reflect Ottoman women's issues, which might have encouraged some male intellectuals to take an active part in the discussion by using female pseudonyms. Ahmet Mithat's extended discussion about Fatma Aliye in his newspaper as an example of an educated Ottoman woman is evidence of such a need.

Conversely, Fatma Aliye's *Nisvân-ı Islâm* (Women of Islam) is a woman's manifesto written by a woman that tries to set a model for the modern Turkish woman. It is structured as a fictional dialogue between Fatma Aliye and her "imagined" European female visitors. In her introduction, she explains the reason that she composed her work: first, she intends to explain

Ottoman society and issues related to women to European travelers because she believes visitors to the city do not witness a true picture of Istanbul. As a woman who spoke French, she considered it to be her responsibility to speak with travelers. Second, she thinks that even Ottoman women do not know much about their history and culture; therefore, they either misunderstand Westernization and become lesser copies of Western women, or they become increasingly conservative and religious. In her fictional representations of herself, she is the role model for the modern Ottoman woman: a Muslim woman with a well-balanced combination of an Eastern and Western education.

Her work in *Nisvân-ı Islâm* and her articles in women's magazines showcase her involvement in women's issues. In their later correspondence, it appears as though Ahmet Mithat noticed this change in Fatma Aliye's writing, and it did not make him happy. She had been his disciple who collaborated with him in constructing his theories of the modern Ottoman woman. In one of his letters, he reminds her that she is not an ordinary woman, saying, "do you need the respect of women? Are you a woman, my dear? If you did not have the morals and position of a man, would your life be enough to produce such works?" (Esen 2014, 100; translation my own). Later, when she starts showing interest in poetry that belonged to a primordial past, he furiously warns her that she must act like a woman: "Why are you doing these evil deeds? Looks like you want to distress me. You haven't given up on being a woman!" (101).

Fatma Aliye never disrespected her mentor but, over time, she adopted a language and taste of her own. In this, she might have been influenced by other women's writing, including that of her sister, Emine Semiye. Ahmet Mithat had not foreseen this change in his student. She showed interest in other women writers, including the famous poet of the nineteenth century, Moralızâde Leylâ Hanım. According to

İbnülemin, she wrote the following passage telling the story of Moralızâde Leylâ's divorce. It is a tongue-in-cheek criticism of their patriarchal world:

> At the wedding night, while Leylâ was in her bridal veil, tinsel and gown, the husband apparently decided to get his new wife used to serve him from the very first night, said: "Wife, come and change this" extending his [injured] arm wrapped in chickpea plaster. Leylâ rushed outside and said to the people around that she would never enter that room again. Her relatives and friends fluttered and tried to persuade her but alas, they could not send the poor girl back to the nuptial chamber. Leylâ said, "I cannot stand to see the face of that man who made me hate chickpea stew all my life." Would not bestowing a girl like Leylâ on a man like him mean to disregard her value and will? They made the helpless Leylâ say these lines:
>
> > Drink in the rose garden, no matter what they say.
> > Enjoy yourself in this world, no matter what they say.
> > What's the difference between slur and praise to me in this world.
> > Let the beloveds live long no matter what they say.
>
> All of that speaking ill of and accusing her, were not to hush her, instead they wanted her to speak. On one hand, they did not want women to read and write but on the other, they wanted, using all of their intelligence and learning, Leylâ to speak up. (translation my own; originally appeared in Havlioğlu 2010a, 41)

Ahmet Mithat and Fatma Aliye's professional collaboration was a product of the nineteenth-century project of modernization. Together, they laid the groundwork for a comparison of men and women's voices and the discussion of gender roles in the changing world. However, this friendship should be evaluated carefully through a historical perspective. Fatma Aliye was not the first woman writer in the intellectual history of Ottoman women who confronted the issues of gender in her later writings. Coming from a long-lived tradition of women's writing, she represents the social and intellectual realities of her time and place.

A close look at Ahmet Mithat's treatment of Fatma Aliye as an intellectual reveals his preconceived ideas of the modern woman. He does not even seem to consider her a woman, but an intellectual. As we know from Mihrî's story, the incongruity between the concepts of the intellectual/poet and the woman is a centuries-old phenomenon. His reaction to Aliye's involvement in the women's movement, for this reason, was outrage.

Fatma Aliye's writing career can be compared to that of Mihrî in terms of her adoption of the dominant discourse at a specific juncture—for Mihrî, the Ottomanization, and for Fatma Aliye, modernization, of the Ottoman intellectual discourse—only to subvert it later from within. While she worked closely with Ahmet Mithat, her articles and novels served the general purpose of Ottoman modernization. She represented the modern Muslim Ottoman woman. However, she surpassed this idealized role through her involvement in the women's movement. Though the women's movement may have originated as part of the Ottoman modernization, it eventually went beyond it. Thus, we see that Fatma Aliye used the authority that she gained through the support of Ahmet Mithat for women's development. For this reason, Fatma Aliye's later writings can be considered subversive.

❀

In a male-dominated field like early modern Ottoman intellectual practice, a woman poet was marginal and, as Mihrî

Hatun demonstrates, this might not have been a negative trait after all. In fact, her marginality could be the source of her subversiveness. As the only woman poet whose poetry has survived, Mihrî appears to be the first and only woman poet until the eighteenth century. As this book has tried to demonstrate, however, she is the only *surviving* example; there is a hidden but consistent tradition of women's writing in Turkish. Mihrî's work is representative of a corpus of texts in intellectual history on and about gender and should be evaluated as such. Because of lack of sources, the somewhat accurate tendency to define each woman intellectual as "the first and only" in her specific time only highlights the dominant discourse's neglect of the consistent existence of marginal female voices throughout history.

Women writers' appropriation of the dominant discourse, on the other hand, is their strategy for survival. It is not a form of imitation. Though a woman writer may seem to be mimicking her male colleagues—besides the fact that imitation was not a bad strategy in early modern times—her work cannot be read in the same way. Women writers in the male-dominant discourses had to take a marginal subject position.

It is not possible to answer some of the questions that emerged from this book because there simply is not enough documentary evidence. Switching the focus from composer to consumer, for instance, we realize that we do not know much about Mihrî's audience other than her immediate circle. Although the extant manuscript copies suggest a readership, we do not know who exactly her readers were. We can only speculate that if women could compose poetry, they could also read and enjoy it. In later periods, we have greater evidence of women's participation in cultural production, both as composers and patrons. It would be interesting to investigate how women poets' works were received. This kind of research will require a comparative approach across time periods. The limits of this book and the new questions it generates are not dead ends; instead, I hope, they are starting points for new avenues of research.

Appendix

❀

Glossary

❀

Bibliography

❀

Index

APPENDIX

Poetry Selection

1.

I composed another pleasant gazel on Ahmet's peach-fuzz script
And wrote it out as a draft on the page of the soul

For years, I rushed about like the wind in a passion for him
In the end, I became a prisoner of his curly locks

In this world, there are many demeaned by his torture and torment
But none other is found so grief stricken as I

The tears from my eyes so flowed in your street that
All its private places were drowned in pearls and beryl

The dulcimer-code of love bent my posture into a harp
And made my body into a wailing and moaning reed flute

His glance quarrels with my life and his eyes with my heart
For it is not uncommon that there is rioting among drunks

The wise is the one who gives his heart to the beauties
He is stupid who does not love the beloved in this world

Let no one in this world bow his neck to the accuser
O Lord, do not let Mihrî be in need of the despicable

As if the arrow of his glance are mirrors in [my] breast
Gives off rays of light in a shield

2.

O my generosity, be the protector (patron) of this fallen one.
For the fame of the noble person are [his] gifts of generosity

Because your court has become a hospital for those who ail
From you, to all who suffer, has come the cure of generosity

By your grace, give medicine to the sick at heart and soul
For by your grace, the essence of generosity will bring them to health

No wonder, the water of your justice gives life to the thirsty-hearted
For your Jesus-breath returns to the dead the soul of generosity

Truly, now the foot of your favor has trod upon my face
Praise God! It will again make pleasant the age of generosity

May you restore the city of Amasya with light
And with your justice, generosity will rebuild every ruined heart

It is time to show mercy to Mihrî, the fallen, with kindness
With your justice, come and take her hand, oh mine of generosity

3.

They have truly given this place the name Göynicek[1]
Its flowing waters give life to the burning hearts

Spring made this area a rose-garden from end to end
Colorful flowers adorned it from dwelling to dwelling

Its herbs hyacinth, its earth ambergris, its water Kevser, its people beautiful
As soon as I saw it I compared it to Paradise

1. Göynicek: a small town in Amasya province.

Day and night its nightingales sing with a pleasant passion
When their voices reach the ear, the heart smiles like a rose

We made it our practice to make pilgrimage to its threshold
On entering we bowed our heads to the place where his foot trod

Mihrî, this is the abode of a saint, whose devotee
You truly are, sincerely, heart and soul

Give praise and prayer for Akşemseddin's[2] eternal reward
He rescues you from sin when he shows concern for you

4.

The trees again adorned themselves in blossoms of every sort
Come now, let us make merry in a rose-garden nook

So what if black passion appears in the head or the heart goes mad?
For the springtime has come and the rivers are all turbid

O heart, why should you cry so about the thorn and its torment?
Look at the beauty of the buds and smile like a (blossoming) rose

Come, it is the time of pleasure, the day of the era of spring
Oh heart, it is time now, you too fill yourself with passion

Facing roses, I have cried out in such a way
That the nightingale's sleep flew away and they all awoke

To bow their faces at the feet of every swaying cypress
My tears were a flowing Oxus[3] wandering the garden

Alas, Mihrî, your life has passed in Amasya
If you are wise, do not go back, stay in Constantinople

2. Akşemseddin: the founder of the Bayramiyye path in Amasya.

3. Oxus River: Amu Darya in Persian and Ceyhun in Turkish. A river in Afghanistan running into the Aral Sea.

5.

Let's cast grief into the sea and be merry on board this ship
Because this world does not endure, let's enjoy this moment

So what if my tears drew me down to the sea?
The wetness had already drowned the little boat of my eye

How much we will weep from the torment of fate's winds?
Let that wind drive us to shore, let us find [there] a friend

Let these heart-sails be filled by the infatuation of love
Let us pull out the anchor of separation and leave the grief behind us

They say to the lover, "Either have patience or make a journey"
The truth of this saying is this: it is the reality of being human

Mihrî, even though the heavens have put you far from your
homeland
The condition of exile is pleasant to many hearts

Don't grieve for your wounded heart for once, a time will come
When you will find a balm for it in the land of exile

6.

My beauty is neither the sun nor is it the new moon
Neither are my eyebrows bows, nor my curl a Royal Signatory

The preacher accused us falsely, calling us beautiful
The number one poets are the biggest liars

It is no surprise if he asks us for a kiss in jest
Anyone whose beard grows in becomes the people's laughing stock

From now on Makâmî, our only kisses will be
Years of angina and the torment of diarrhea

At every door one grovels begging for a kiss
Inside the gate, Mihrî herself begging of you

7.

In this world, who among the beauties is enough for you
Yet, [being] a mad, suffering lover is enough for me

To prolong loving you each night in the heart's monk-cell
Having my soul for a proof and my skin for a mat is enough

As for holding back, my tears have exceeded all bounds from the start
As for injustice, for my soul it's sufficient, oh heart-thief, enough

In this world, I see only suffering from you, the rival sees your favors
If this is [done] to kill the lover, then, o faithless one, it is enough

Groveling on my face, with their footprints I became acquainted
With your dogs in your street and for this afflicted one it is enough

Oh Necâtî, you want a reed mat for a mattress
For Mihrî, just a place on the beloved's threshold is enough

With a single seed [for bait], his curl hunted the heart-bird
As long as I live in this world, this will be food enough for me

8.

My time passed with groans and sighs in a night of grief
Never once was I the companion of that moon-faced one

O heavens, what crime did I commit against you, even once
That you never let me be friends with that black-haired one?

My friend, what the heart now suffers in separation's grief
Only I and God alone know what it is

Separation from you, O faithless, has brought my soul into my throat.
O beloved! One day, it will surely exit with a sigh for your sake

If it is a sin among you, the pious ones, to love the beauties
Then don't bother yourself, leave me to burn with that sin

Don't fail to beware the gazes of the lovely ones
They have led a thousand *şeyhs* astray with single glance

O Mihrî, you compose a parallel to a poem by Necâtî
But you are a beggar and bankrupt and he the companion of a
ruler

9.

As brilliant lyrics reached us from that beloved
Jesus-like, a breath of life reached my dead body

Your sweet lip's Ferhad[4] became crazy at heart for it
He would give up life and this world but never give it up

Parted from you, I bent my body like a signet
I was hit on the head by a stone of reproach made of coral

When the morning breeze comes to the rose-bed of your cheek,
beloved,
The whole world smells sweetly of hyacinth and sweet herbs (basil)

My dear, since I saw you, o lord of beauties, in your street
I have had no desire for Paradise and have given up beautiful boys

He is ignorant, vastly clownish and ignorant
Who does not consider you superior to Selmân-ı Sâvecî[5]

4. Ferhad: one of the main characters in the story of Ferhad and Şirîn. He was in love with Şirîn, the beloved of Hüsrev, the Persian king. Upon Şirîn's request, he carves a passage in Mount Behistun.

5. Selmân-ı Sâvecî: the great Persian poet (1309–79), famous for his odes.

O Hâtemî, you lied Mihrî when you played the lover
By God, she loves you better than any boy

10.

O Güvâhî, in this world may God
Make you addicted to a beloved

Like a nightingale in the garden of the beloved's cheek
Sigh with cries and moans

Let him put the rope of his locks about your neck
And make in his dimple a prison-pit for you

Let him light the wick of your soul in the night of grief
Let a world's [the drinking party's] sun and moon burn bright

Let his lip remind you of his cup of wine
And his neck of an ewer in the gathering

Ever let the black eye of the bow-brows
Drink your blood instead of water

At last, let him hang you on the tip of his locks
That monarch of the domain of loveliness

If you ask openly about the reason for this poem
And you inquire, saying, "What is Güvâhî's sin?"

It is that you did not mention
Mihrî in a few couplets now and again

11.

Because God sent you on your way with fortune
May God make you the love-addict of another shah
Let us not keep you, go to what you prayed for at early morn
Go, my lord, go, I leave you in the hands of God

Once you were İskender[6] in Amasya town
Like Hızr[7] you were a guide to seekers for the water of life
O idol, you were chief among the beauties too
Go, my lord, go, I leave you in the hands of God

Let us go to your street, moaning all the time
Let the river of my tears flow into every stream
Let us bow our face to your threshold and make it our own
Go, my lord, go, I leave you in the hands of God

How about that time when you were intimate with us night and day
You were a balm to our wounded heart
O my dear sir, you were a man too
Go, my lord, go, I leave you in the hands of God

Alas, until my eyes see you once again
We will pass our days and nights sighing and weeping
When our hearts reach our throats, let this be our words
Go, my lord, go, I leave you in the hands of God

When the chest made itself a target for your bow-brows
You would shoot glance arrows at the target-pot of heart and soul
Go to others, my crazy heart will not forget you
Go, my lord, go, I leave you in the hands of God

Because the heavens separated us when we were friends
The aching heart burnt brands on top of wounds

6. İskender: either the historical figure of Alexander the Great or the İskender-i Zülkarneyn, both of whom are mentioned in the Qur'an. In terms of Mihrî's story, İskender also refers to one of her companions.

7. Hızr: a mythical character who drank the *ab-ı hayat*, or water of life, and became immortal. He is mentioned in the story of İskender as a companion to İskender during his journey to the underworld in search of immortality. In folklore, he is believed to have helped people in need.

O friend, your memory and image remain with us as a gift
Go, my lord, go, I leave you in the hands of God

Let autumn not come to the garden of your beauty, oh tulip-cheek
Why grieve, for you there are a thousand like Mihrî every day
In the end, it is your custom to remember friends
Go, my lord, go, I leave you in the hands of God

12.

I opened my eyes from sleep suddenly and raised my head
I saw, standing before me, a moon-faced heart-stealer

I believe my lucky star rose or else I attained mystical power
For in my quarter, I saw Jupiter rise in the night

I saw divine light flow from his beauty, although plainly
He looks like a Muslim but his dress is an infidel's

As I opened and closed my eyes, he vanished from my sight
And I discerned that he was either angel or fairy

Having reached the water of life, Mihrî will not die 'til the
    Resurrection
Because she saw İskender clearly in the darkness of night

13.

While the nightingale of the soul rejoiced in you, rosebud-mouth
It took no pleasure in a paradise-like garden in this world

O masters of pleasure, strive to pass your lives with love
If you wish, with all your heart, to find pleasure in this world

Let your bow-brows shoot the arrows of your eyelashes, oh beloved
This heart and soul of mine take pleasure in that bow and arrows

Did they suppose that your beard spoiled your beauty's flower
    garden?
Don't the masters of pure pleasure always rejoice in the autumn?

His eye said, "Let me plunder Mihrî's life"
Let it, indeed we will greatly rejoice in that loss

14.

This my cruel beloved was my darling once upon a time
With his deceitful eyes, he was lovely and pleasing once upon a time

His rose-cheeks laughed and kings were their slaves
His early peach was popular once upon a time

His eyebrow was a bow, what it hunted were lives
He was a bud-mouth, much desired once upon a time

Lives were sacrificed to him, yet he wouldn't look one of them in the face
His lovers were all excited to the point of sacrifice once upon a time

Now, as Mihrî sees his beard upon his cheek, she says
This my cruel beloved was my darling once upon a time

15.

Our eyes once again saw a moon-face and fell in love with it
Our eyes met in sideways glances and we cast ourselves into the flames

I'd give my life to ask the description of his lip
But we don't have the courage to ask for what we want

Around his cheek, his locks give us long life
Cheered by it, our days and nights become as one

We get along with the rival, clinging to his skirts
But even though we beg, our words are not worth a scrap

Let us be one and the same as dirt on the path of his love
Let us destroy the domain of life and let our dust rise to the sky

The heavenly host wafts our sighs to the sky day and night
It's a wonder that the stars are not set aflame by the lightning bolt
of our sighs

O Mihrî, we are moths to the candle of his cheek
Let us blaze up and burn, a hundred of us aren't worth a cent

16.

How much respect should I show to [my] rivals for the beloved's
sake?
How much should I plead to a thousand thorns for just one rose?

Wherever you look, it is the thorn that holds the bud to its breast
I've become incapable of going to a rose-bed, oh my friends

The thorn of jealousy rends my heart a thousand times in an instant
Have I only myself as a companion for weeping and wailing?

My lips said, let her not allow her secret [of love] out of her mouth
I'd give my head rather than reveal this secret [even] to a hermit

He turns away when he sees me and prefers the rival
I don't know what I did to that beloved, except to love him

That heart-thief swore to hang me from his lovelocks
With all my heart, I'm content to be hung on that gallows

Among the people, I am Mihrî, among the lovers, I am ordinary
But in the beloved's presence, I am weak and wretched and helpless

17.

Would that I had never been depicted in the manner of this existence
Would that I had never come into this world and had been
non-existent

I spent my life ever buffeted by the winds of destiny
Ah, would that I had eternally been deprived of this life

Being praised for poverty and humility in every regard
Would then that I had been served with respect and kind words

Rather than being a nightingale in the business of the heart and crying always
It would have been lovely had I been an owl [living] in the ruins

The soul ever lives with torment in the dwelling of woe
Would that I had been left destitute and never reached this day

Though everyone thinks me famous for all of this knowledge
Would that I had been reviled for all kinds of ignorance

For the people of the time being a Turk is an honor
Would that I were garlic in their sour tarhana soup

Whenever the turning sphere gives the ignorant all they desire
Would that I, your servant Mihrî, were known for ignorance

18.

Although I could not write out the inscription of your beauty
I have, instead, read often from the holy verse of your loveliness

Since time began, the one who does commentary on loving you told me
Observe the exegesis of your lip and [in it] the guidance of God

Even though it was difficult, I still memorized in my heart
The [tangled] problems of your hair and the peculiarities of your face

The heart always proclaims a sermon in the name of your beauty
For now it makes the moral argument for it in this world

Leave off the story of his locks and recite from the holy text of his beauty
If you wish to do away with the [dark and twisted] errors of heart and soul

May God grant that one day I might see
The beloved giving up tyranny and ending his oppression

He shoos me away like a dog and detains the rival with kisses
See the concern he shows to him, and the kind of politeness shown
to me

O my lord, when his monarch oppresses a person
To whose gate can he go and make his complaint

How can one know the story of Mihrî, who has not read
Her petition on the grief of your torment and cruelty?

19.

I've come, rubbing my face in the dirt, making my way right to you
Oh monarch, I wish I might reveal my sorry plight to you

Of all the world's kings, you are the king so famed for justice
That the sun comes to your door each day in service to you

O you rose-cheek, the nightingale of the soul recites
Praises day and night, at dawn and dusk to you

O my lord, the fire of jealousy has consumed this thirsty heart in
flames
Don't leave me in the darkness of grief, let Hızr be a companion to
you

O Mihrî, let it make you as youthful as Züleyhâ[8]
Should the monarch turn his Joseph-like gaze to you

8. Züleyhâ: one of the main characters of the Yusuf (Joseph) and Züleyhâ story. In the Old Testament and the Qur'an, she is mentioned as the wife of Aziz. In the literary versions of this love story, she gains a name, becomes one of the main characters, and pursues Yusuf throughout her life. In the end, when she is old and blind from crying for the love of Yusuf, he finally looks at her and she gains her youth and eyes back.

20.

We are among those who came to sacrifice our lives for the beloved's sake
We have become the seekers after pain, among those who came for a cure

We are among those who came manfully to the playing field of love
That might make my head a ball for the mallet of your love locks

I tell you truly, in my heart I hold tight your love
I am among those who came to the rope faithfully, like Mansur

In every nook of your beauty's flower garden, my beloved friend
I am among those who came to be singing nightingales and to cry out

I've come to say "Thank God" for the alms of your loveliness
My dear, do not think this dervish is among those who come for bread

O heart's physician, it is time to cure me with restraints
I am among those who came crazy for the chains of your locks

O Mihrî, for the candle of the beloved's cheek, always
Let me burn like a moth, for I am among those who came on fire

21.

If you are a lover, leave your virtue and modesty aside for love's sake
Strive on this path, give your life to it, else you will lose the beloved

If you want to have your beloved casually, without really desiring it
Don't be heedless, watch out, for your beauty will belong to another

If you should drown the world, no one will wipe away your tears
Even though you weep blood, crying piteously, a thousand times a day

Cry out while you are in the flower garden of that rosebud
Or else tomorrow the rose will go and you remain, oh poor
nightingale

To save the heart-holder's skirts from the hand of the thorn
Why don't you prostrate yourself to every flowerbed and beg

O help! If you are manly, it is time to strive and drive off the rival
Exert yourself that the thorn not grasp the fresh rose's skirts

Look now! For a time Mihrî would wander the heavens
But see, because of this she has [now] become dust underfoot

22.

My love, from the design of your face, the heart learned to paint
From the sun of your loveliness, the world was filled with
illumination

I wonder if the ruby took [its] color from your pure ruby lip
For the pearl learned roundness from the dot of your mouth

Although scent in this world is always the musk of Khotan[9]
The perfumer's craft was taught to it by the scent of your hair

Although God created rose-faced heart-thieves in this world
In your person he gathered together beauty, freshness, and youth

They say your rival boasts and says, "I'll kill her one day"
If he's a man, let him come and I'll show manliness to that
unmanly coward

What matter, if Mihrî should risk her life on the battlefield of love
for you
At times your glance was a sword to her and your curl made a hoop

9. Khotan: a city in northern China. In Persian and Ottoman poetry, musk is associated with this city, likely because it was on the Silk Road.

23.

Revolving fate kindly gave us a hand the other night
Heart-thief and beloved joined us for a chat the other night

I had been left in the dark of night with abundant woes
And a gleaming moon dropped into my hands the other night

A heart-ravisher, lord of the land of beauty, favored me
He came to me, his beggar, as a visitor the other night

Standing on one foot the candle of the bedroom burned
Till morn, impassioned by the beloved's image, the other night

He adorned the gathering with the fineness of his beauty
That young beard, that mole, that unruly hair, the other night

Grown ardent, drunk with desire for a rosebud-ruby
Mihrî, tore the collar of her robes the other night

24.

I wandered the wilderness with my beloved this night
It is required that I give myself over to gratitude this night

We were many friends mounted on the steed of fortune
The field of play was ours from end to end this night

With the sword of wrath we split in two the rival's head
Yes, the ball and mallet were in our hands this night

He pulled the cloud of hair away and exposed his cheek
The gleaming moon became our intimate this night

I was already drunk with his love's wine, he offered another drink
And one sip of his ruby lip bewildered me this night

The accuser strove to forbid me my beloved
Yet, no matter what you say, Satan could not seduce him this night

Thanks be to God, the rival was excluded from among us
So no separation intruded on our private moments this night

Because he let us circumambulate the Ka'ba[10] of his beauty
I sacrificed my heart and soul a thousand times this night

The fifteenth of the month of Zilhicce[11] was a lovely night
For Mihrî wandered about with her beloved on this night

25.

A physician was our confidant again this night
He gave balm to our ailing heart this night

Our hearts were wounded by his glance-arrows
Yet his ruby salved that wound again this night

For long we had suffered the torments of fate
God be praised, that beloved dispelled our grief this night

We relaxed in that idol's gathering until dawn
Each moment passed with a thousand pleasures this night

While opportunity offers its hand, embrace and kiss the beloved
They do not always fall into our hands, Mihrî, this party, this night

26.

I was hoping he would come with his tousled hair tonight
That I would make my soul a moth to his cheek's candle tonight

10. Ka'ba: a building in the Masjid al-Haram in Mecca and a site of pilgrimage. Muslims turn in the direction of the Ka'ba when they worship.

11. Zilhicce: the last month of the Islamic calendar and the month of pilgrimage.

Suddenly a host of ugly people entered and I said,
"Did Solomon[12] loose his monsters on us tonight?"

A troop made for hanging gathered at the party
I wonder where to find a rope for them tonight

Some were bald, some blind, some halt and lame
Whom did revolving fate make our companions tonight?

Look what the heavens did to Mihrî on the longest of nights
It was heedless, brought them in, made them our guests tonight

27.

Tonight, in a high palace with a royal falcon
We made merry with moonlight and lute 'til morn

In the Wheel, let Venus play her harp and castanets for Earth
Whenever those moon-faces sing out with voices raised

It bent my body into a harp, and set things "Straight" in the melody
It drew my skin into a string, made the "Lovers" happy with the
"Lord's Allure"[13]

In the elite gathering of the Solomon of this age, beautiful faces
With ambergris locks serve pleasantly with charm

I saw that suspended palace of peerless construction
And thought it the Hüma[14] soaring in the sky

12. Solomon: Süleyman the prophet is described as having the ability to communicate with animals and supernatural beings, such as jinn and monsters.

13. The following terms are translations of the musical modes in classical Turkish music: the Straight, mode of Rast; the Lovers, mode of Uşşak; and Lord of Allure, mode of Şehnaz.

14. Hüma: bird of fortune. According to myth, people would gather in a courtyard and whoever's head this bird landed on would be the next sultan.

O Mihrî, thank God he remembered you and you chatted
Tonight, in a high palace with a royal falcon

28.

The rose again showed a beloved's cheek to the flowerbed
Take care, oh sorrowful bird, don't be silent but laugh instead

Keep to the fields for the days of spring will pass away
Don't let the chance slip by for the rose will not stay

O Sâkî,[15] bring unmixed wine in a goblet of glass
For the nightingale and its song and the rosy-cheeked rose will pass

In the season of the rose, come to the garden and make merry
All the beauties hold bunches of roses in their hands

Amid the greenery, the narcissus is drunk on the image of your eye
And look there, the rose is waiting for the bud to smile

The spring of time reaches the point of becoming autumn
Take care, for the rose will tear and tatter its petals

Pass your life happily, Mihrî, for the days of roses will come to a close
And you'll say, "Where is the nightingale and where the springtime rose?"

29.

The days of spring arrived again and decorated every land
The creator adorned the horizons with blossoms

Look how that artist painted with all his artistry and again
From every naked tree displayed a beauty's face

15. Sâkî: cupbearer, distributor of water/wine, and a spiritual teacher.

Good luck is theirs who may be in the flower garden now
In one hand the wine goblet, in the other the beloved's locks

Now let him take a rose from his cheek, then wine from his lip,
Now let him embrace his waist, then sit close and kiss him

Like a rose, he came again today with the springtime of the world
He revealed his face to the flowerbed just like the sovereign

The cypresses saw his heart-ravishing body and began to dance
The plane tree became aroused at this and clapped its hand

Come drink unmixed wine to desire for every rose-body
If you are wise, beware, do not miss this moment

Mihrî said, "Is there any nightingale like me for that rose?"
And it said, "I see a thousand (nightingales) like you every day."

30.

It is the season of spring, the moment of the flower garden is here
Nightingale of the heart, now your wailing will increase, come, it's time

Let us go and in the rose garden terrace let us observe
The heart-holder's cypress gait and the way he sways

If, perhaps, we touched a rose-cheek, bud-mouth
We endured the tyranny and torment of a thousand thorns

Let us make our breast a drum, our body a harp
Let the beloved hear what the cycles of the musical modes are

If all the people of the world accuse us, what woe in that,
If the beloved has but an atom's faithfulness to us

Just let the skirt of union with the beloved come into my hand
And I would bend my neck to the rival's sword of disaster

Although you lack many gazels, recalling the beloved's lip
O Mihrî, your sweet speech checkmates the parrot

31.

Circulate the wine, o Saki, let us delight in spring
Blossom time is come, let us delight in being close

Today, which is the rose season, in the meadow, with the nightingale
Let us shout and wail, let us delight in sighs and cries

What to do? The thorn never lets go of the rose's skirts
So for the rose's sake, let us just delight in the thorn

I said, "For your sake, I brought my soul as a gift, my dear sir"
He said, "Bring it here, let us delight in whatever you have"

Let go of this world and life for the beloved's sake, Mihrî
He called you "my dog," so let us delight in this esteem

32.

Two silver bodies rode on the horse of fortune
As if, to the world's people, one was soul, the other body

One the İskender of the age, the other Hayder Şah[16]
Could the castle of the body endure their swords of power?

Clearly one is an angel, one a seraph
As one would observe who was there at the time

Mihrî, no one sees [experiences] their love except for the rival
What can we do with a person who turns everything to good luck?

16. Hayder Şah: a fifteenth-century Sufi *şeyh* of the Turkmens in Anatolia. He was the son of Şeyh Cüneyd, founder of Safeviyye path, and the father of Shah İsmail, founder of the Safevid dynasty in Iran.

What a blessed day was the Feast of Sacrifice, I took delight
Two silver bodies rode on the horse of fortune

33.

Thus did I recognize the beloved after the festival
His cure overcame my ailment after the festival

I wonder what will happen if I don't sink a tooth into
The sugar-pie of the beloved's pure ruby [lip] after the festival

He is wise who would watch the graceful ones
And make a tour of every nook and cranny after the festival

Souls rock in the swing of the beauties' locks
When they adorn the square of their loveliness after the festival

Say, "Let the rival not expect to swing with that beloved
Look, there is a rope ready for him to swing on after the festival"

Really, Mihrî was a sacrifice for the festival of union with him
But she surrendered her life to the beloved after the festival

We have attained many blessed moments but in truth
There won't be the like of that time, alas, where are the days after
the festival?

34.

At every moment, good health is fitting for you, the blessed one
At every instant, comfort is fitting for that pure body of yours

In a sublime dwelling, night and day, with joy and pleasure
Converse with a lovely woman in the health-fitting courtyard

May pain be distant from that delicate body of yours,
For your enemy, torment in the house of grief is fitting

Why does a fever grip you, let it grip your infidel rival
For you, good health, for your enemy, pain and degradation are
fitting

In order to cut off the head of your enemy with the sword of wrath
For your boldness and for your arm, strength are fitting

May the one who envies you ever wail like the reed-flute
For you, merrymaking with harp and dulcimer is fitting

May God spare your life for your mother
Whose one and only you are, for you, eminence is fitting

Praise God, Mihrî, your well-wisher could visit you
Those who see you say, "To you, [such] pillars of prosperity are
fitting"

Glossary of Terms

bey	a male title applied to high administrative officers in early modern times
çelebi	a title applied to educated men
divan	poetry collection
efendi	an informal title applied to economic or intellectual elite men
gazel	lyric poem
ḥadith	the sayings or actions attributed to the Prophet Muhammad
hatun	a title of respect given to privileged women in the early modern period; replaced with *hanım* by the nineteenth century
hoca	teacher, professor
imam	Muslim community leader
kadı	magistrate
kasîde	ode
mahlas	pen name
meclis	gathering, either for social purposes or entertainment
medrese	higher-education institutes for men in Islamic societies
mesnevî	narrative poem
müderris	professor at a higher-education institution
musâhib	boon-companion
nazîre	parallel poem
risâle	treatise

şehzâde	crown prince
şeyh	religious/spiritual authority
sıbyan mektepleri	primary schools
sunnah	custom or practices of the Prophet Muhammad contained in the *ḥadith*
sura	Qur'anic verse
tezkire	biographical dictionary

Bibliography

Manuscript Sources

Mihrî Hâtun Dîvanı, Ali Emiri, 414, Fatih Millet Library, Istanbul.
Mihrî Hâtun Dîvanı, 3974 Ayasofya, Süleymaniye Library, Istanbul.
Mihrî Hâtun Dîvanı, TY 1994/2, Istanbul Univ. Library.
Mihrî Hâtun Dîvanı, 220, National Library, Ankara.

Encyclopedia

İslam Ansiklopedisi (DIA). Istanbul: Türkiye Diyanet Vakfı İslam Araştırmaları Merkezi, 2014.

Published Sources

Ahmed, Leila. 1992. *Women and Gender in Islam: Historical Roots of Modern Debate.* New Haven, CT: Yale Univ. Press.

Ali, Samer. 2010. *Arabic Literary Salons in the Islamic Middle Ages.* Notre Dame, IN: Univ. of Notre Dame Press.

Andrews, Walter. 1985. *Poetry's Voice, Society's Song: Ottoman Lyric Poetry.* Seattle: Univ. of Washington Press.

Andrews, Walter, and Mehmet Kalpaklı. 2005. *The Age of Beloveds: Love and the Beloved in Early-Modern Ottoman and European Culture and Society.* Durham, NC: Duke Univ. Press.

Andrews, Walter, Mehmet Kalpaklı, and Najaat Black. 2006. *Ottoman Lyric Poetry: An Anthology.* Seattle: Univ. of Washington Press.

Âşık Çelebi. 2010. *Meşâʿirü'ş-Şuaʿrâ.* Edited by Filiz Kılıç. Istanbul: İstanbul Araltırmaları Enstitüsü.

Babayan, Kathryn. 1998. "The *ʿAqā'id al-Nisā*: A Glimpse at Safevid Women in Local Isfahani Culture." In *Women in the Medieval Islamic World*, edited by Gavin Hambly, 349–81. New York: Palgrave Macmillan.

Bates, Ülkü. 1978. "Women as Patrons of Architecture in Turkey." In *Women in the Muslim World*, edited by Lois Beck and Nikki Keddie, 245–60. Cambridge, MA: Harvard Univ. Press.

de Beauvoir, Simone. (1949) 1993. *The Second Sex*. Translated by H. M. Parshley. London: Everyman.

Behar, Cem. 2012. *Aşk Olmayınca Meşk Olmaz: Geleneksel Osmanlı Türk Müziğinde Öğretim ve İntikal*. Istanbul: Yapı Kredi Yayınları.

Behrens-Abouseif, Doris. 1999. *Beauty in Arabic Culture*. Princeton, NJ: Princeton Univ. Press.

Bekiroğlu, Nazan. 1999. "Osmanlıda Kadın Şairler." In *Osmanlı*, vol. 9, 802–12. Ankara: Yeni Türkiye Yayınları.

Berkey, Jonathan. 1992. *The Transmission of Knowledge in Medieval Cairo: A Social History of Islamic Education*. Princeton, NJ: Princeton Univ. Press.

Brookshaw, Dominic. 2005. "Odes of a Poet-Princess: The Ghazals of Jahān-Malik Khātūn." *Iran* 43: 173–95.

Brown, Judith, and Robert Davis, eds. 1998. *Gender and Society in Renaissance Italy*. New York: Routledge.

Butler, Judith. 1988. "Performative Acts and Gender Constitution: An Essay in Phenomenology and Feminist Theory." *Theatre Journal* 40 (4): 519–31.

———. 1990. *Gender Trouble: Feminism and the Subversion of Identity*. London: Routledge.

Çavuşoğlu, Mehmed. 1971. *Necati Bey Divanının Tahlili*. Istanbul: Milli Eğitim Basımevi.

———. 1978. "16. Yüzyılda yaşamış bir kadın şair Nisayi." *Tarih Enstitüsü Dergisi* 9: 405–16.

cooke, miriam. 2010. *Nazira Zeineddin: A Pioneer of Islamic Feminism*. Oxford: Oneworld.

Cunbur, Müjgân. 1988. "İmadu'l-cihad ve XVI yüzyıl kadın şairlerinden Ayşe Hubbî kadın." In *Türk tarih kongresi bildirileri*, 901–3. Ankara: Türk Tarih Kurumu.

Elias, Jamal. 2012. *Aisha's Cushion: Religious Art, Perception, and Practice in Islam*. Cambridge, MA: Harvard Univ. Press.

Erünsal, İsmail E. 1981. "II. Bāyezid devrine ait bir in'āmāt defteri." *Tarih Enstitüsü Dergisi* 10–11: 303–42.

———. 1983. *The Life and Works of Taci-zade Ca'fer Celebi, with a Critical Edition of His Divan*. Istanbul: Edebiyat Fakultesi Basimevi.

Esen, Nüket. 2014. *Hikaye Anlatan Adam: Ahmet Mithat*. Istanbul: İletişim.

Evliyâ Çelebi. 2003. *Evliyâ Çelebi Seyahatnâmesi*. Edited by Yücel Dağlı, Seyit Ali Kahraman, and Robert Dankoff. 8 vols. Istanbul: Yapı Kredi Yayınları.

Faroqhi, Suraiya. 2000. *Subjects of Sultan*. London: Tauris.

Fatma Aliye Hanım. 2012. *Muhadarat*. Istanbul: Özgür Yayınları.

Felek, Özgen. 2014. *Kitabü'l-Menâmât: Sultan Murad'ın Rüya Mektupları*. Istanbul: Tarih Vakfı Yurt Yayınları.

Fetvacı, Emine. 2012. "The Album of Ahmed I." *Ars Orientalis* 42: 127–38.

Gibb, E. J. W. 1900–1909. *A History of Ottoman Poetry*. 6 vols. London: Luzac.

Goffman, Daniel. 2002. *The Ottoman Empire and the Early Modern Europe*. Cambridge: Cambridge Univ. Press.

Gruendler, Beatrice. 2010. *Medieval Arabic Praise Poetry: Ibn Al-Rumi and the Patron's Redemption*. London: Routledge.

Gülbadan. 1944. *Hümanyunname*. Edited by A. S. Beveridge and Yusuf Hikmet Bayur. Ankara: Türk Tarih Kurumu.

Gündüz, Erol. 2009. "Divan ve Halk Edebiyatı Sanatçılarına İlham Kaynağı Olan Rüya." *Selçuk Üniversitesi Sosyal Bilimler Enstitüsü Dergisi* 22: 187–202.

Havlioğlu, Didem. 2007. "Osmanlı Şiirinde Kadının Sesi: Mihri Hatun'un Hatime-yi Risalesi ve Necati'ye bir naziresi." In *In*

Memoriam Şinasi Tekin I: Journal of Turkish Studies 31, edited by Yücel Dağlı, Yorgos Dedes, and Selim Kuru, 37–46. Cambridge, MA: Harvard Univ. Press.

———. 2010a. "On the Margins and Between the Lines: Ottoman Women Poets from 15th to 20th Century." *Turkish Historical Review* 1: 25–54.

———. 2010b. "Valideler, Hemşireler, Kerimeler: Osmanlı Şiirinde Kadınlararasılık." *Journal of Turkish Studies: Festschirift in Honor of Walter Andrews* 34/II: 105–15.

———. 2015a. "Estetik Hafıza Olarak Telmih: Süreklilik ve Başkalaşım" [Telmih as an Aesthetic Memory: Continuity and Change]. *Monograf: edebiyat eleştirisi dergisi* 4: 10–30.

———. 2015b. "The Magic of a Joke: Humor and Gender in Islamicate Ottoman Aesthetics." In *Laughter, Humor, and the (Un)making of Gender: Historical and Cultural Perspectives*, edited by Anna Foka and Jonas Liliequist, 136–58. New York: Palgrave MacMillan.

Havlioğlu, Didem, and Hatice Aynur. 2013. "Medhiyenin Cinsiyeti: Kadınlara Yazılmış Kasideler" [Gender of the Ode: Qasidas Written for Women]. In *Eski Türk Edebiyatı Çalışmaları/ Kasideye Medhiyye: biçime, işleve ve muhtevaya ait tespitler*, 76–123. Istanbul: Klâsik.

Hızlı, Mefail. 2001. "Osmanlı Sıbyan Mekteplerine Göre Okutulan Dersler." In *Osmanlı Dünyasında Bilim ve Eğitim: Milletlerarası Kongresi: Tebliğler*, 109–15. Istanbul: Research Center for Islamic History, Art and Culture (IRCICA).

Holbrook, Victoria. 1994. *The Unreadable Shores of Love: Turkish Modernity and Mystic Romance*. Austin: Univ. of Texas Press.

Homerin, Th. Emil, ed. 2011. *Emanations of Grace: Mystical Poems by ʿĀʾishah al-Bāʿūnīyya (d. 923/1517)*. Louisville, KY: Fons Vitae.

Hüsameddin, Hüseyin. 1986. *Amasya Tarihi*. 5 vols. Amasya: Amasya Valiliği Yayınları.

İnalcık, Halil. 2001. *The Ottoman Empire Classical Age: 1300–1600*. Phoenix: Phoenix Press.

———. 2010. *Şair ve Patron: Patrimonyal Devlet ve Sanat Üzerine Sosyolojik Bir İnceleme.* Ankara: Doğu Batı.

———. 2011. *Has-bağçede ʿayş u tarab: Nedimler, Şairler, Mutripler.* Istanbul: Türkiye İş Bankası Yayınları.

Jones, Ann Rosalind. 1986. "City Women and Their Audiences: Louise Labé and Veronica Franco." In *Rewriting the Renaissance: The Discourses of Sexual Difference in Early Modern Europe*, edited by Margaret W. Ferguson, Maureen Quilligan, and Nancy Vickers, 299–316. Chicago: Univ. of Chicago Press.

———. 1990. *Currency of Eros: Women's Love Lyric in Europe, 1540–1620.* Bloomington: Indiana Univ. Press.

———. 2007. "Writing the Body: Toward an Understanding of l'Ecriture Feminine." In *Feminisms: An Anthology of Literary Theory and Criticism*, 2nd ed., edited by Robyn R. Warhol and Diane Price Herndl, 370–84. New Brunswick, NJ: Rutgers Univ. Press.

Kafadar, Cemal. 1993. "Women in Seljuk and Ottoman Society up to the Mid-9th Century." In *9000 Years of the Anatolian Women*, 192–201. Istanbul: Turkish Republic Ministry of Culture, General Directorate of Monuments and Museums.

———. 1994. *Rüya Mektupları: Asiye Hatun.* Istanbul: Oğlak.

———. 2007. "Introduction: A Rome of One's Own: Reflections on Cultural Geography and Identity in the Lands of Rum." *Muqarnas* 24: 7–25.

Kalpaklı, Mehmet. 2006. "Osmanlı Şiir Akademisi: Nazire." In *Türk Edebiyatı Tarihi*, vol. 2, 135–39. Ankara: Kültür ve Turizm Bakanlığı Yayınları.

Kappert, Petra. 1976. *Die osmanischen Prinzen und ihre Residenz Amasya im 15. und 16. Jahrhundert.* Leiden: Nederlands Historisch-Archaeologisch Instituut te Istanbul.

Karakaya-Stump, Ayfer. 2003. "Debating Progress in a 'Serious Newspaper for Muslim Women': The Periodical Kadın of the Post-revolutionary Salonica, 1908–1909." *British Journal of Middle Eastern Studies* 30 (2): 155–81.

Karataş, Hasan. 2011. "The City as a Historical Actor: The Urbanization and Ottomanization of the Halvetiye Sufi Order by the City of Amasya in the Fifteenth and Sixteenth Centuries." PhD diss., Univ. of California, Berkeley.

Kazan, Hilal. 2010. *16. Asırda Sarayın Sanatı Himayesi*. Istanbul: İsar Vakfı Yayınları.

———. 2014. *Dünden Bugüne Hanım Hattatlar*. Istanbul: Büyükşehir Belediyesi Yayınları.

Kınalızâde Âlî Çelebi. 2012. *Ahlâk-ı Alâî*. Edited by Mustafa Koç. Istanbul: Klâsik.

Kınalızâde Hasan Çelebi. 1989. *Tezkiretü'ş-Şuara*. Edited by İsmet Parmaksızoğlu. Ankara: Türk Tarih Kurumu.

Kızıltan, Mübeccel. 1994. "Dîvân edebiyatı özelliklerine uyarak şiir yazan kadın şailer." *Sombahar* 21/22: 104–69.

Kristeva, Julia. 1984. *Revolution in Poetic Language*. New York: Columbia Univ. Press.

Küçük, Sabahattin. 1994. *Bakî Divanı*. Ankara: Türk Dil Kurumu Yayınları.

Kurnaz, Cemal. 1999. "Osmanlı Tarihinde İz Bırakan Amasyalı Bir Aile: Müeyyedzadeler." In *Türkiye-Orta Asya Edebi İlişkileri*, 647–67. Ankara: Akçağ.

Kuru, Selim. 2000. "A Sixteenth Century Scholar: Deli Birader and His Dāfi′ü'l-gumūm ve rāfi′ü'l-humūm." PhD diss., Harvard Univ.

———. 2006. "Naming the Beloved in Ottoman Turkish Gazel: The Case of İshak Çelebi (d. 1537/8)." In *Ghazal as World Literature II. From a Literary Genre to a Great Tradition. The Ottoman Gazel in Context*, edited by Angelika Neuwirth, Michael Hess, Judith Pfeiffer, and Börte Sagaster, 163–73. Würzburg: Ergon-Verlag GmbH.

———. 2007. "Sex in the Text: Deli Birader and Ottoman Literary Canon." *Middle Eastern Literatures* 10: 157–74.

Latîfî. 2000. *Tezkiretü'ş-Şu'arâ: inceleme, metin*. Edited by Rıdvan Canım. Ankara: Atatürk Kültür Merkezi.

Lewis, Franklin. 1995. "Reading, Writing and Recitation: Sanā'ī and the Origins of the Persian Ghazal." PhD diss., Univ. of Chicago.

Makdisi, George. 2012. *Ortaçağda Yüksek Öğretim: İslam Dünyası ve Hıristiyan Batı.* Istanbul: Klasik.

Malti-Douglas, Fedwa. 1992. *Woman's Body, Woman's Word: Gender and Discourse in Arabo-Islamic Writing.* Princeton, NJ: Princeton Univ. Press.

Mehmed Zihnî. 1877. *Meşâhirü'n-Nisâ*, vol. 2, 240–41. Istanbul: Matbaa-i Amire.

Mengi, Mine. 2010. *Divan Şiiri Yazıları.* Ankara: Akçağ.

Mihrî Hatun. 1967. *Mihrî Hâtun Divanı.* Edited by Elena Mashtakova. Moscow: Asya Halklar Enstitüsü.

———. 2007. *Mihrî Hâtun Divanı.* Edited by Mehmet Arslan. Amasya: Amasya Valiliği Yayınları.

Müstakimzade Süleyman Sadeddin Efendi. 1928. *Tuhfe-i Hattatin.* Istanbul: Devlet Matbaası.

Najmabadi, Afsaneh. 1999. "Reading—and Enjoying—'Wiles of Women' Stories as a Feminist." *Iranian Studies* 32 (2): 203–22.

———. 2005. *Women with Mustaches and Men without Beards: Gender and Sexual Anxieties of Iranian Modernity.* Berkeley: Univ. of California Press.

Najmabadi, Afsaneh, and Gayane Karen Merguerian. 1997. "Zulaykha and Yusuf: Whose Best Story?" *International Journal of Middle East Studies* 29 (4): 485–508.

Necâtî. 1963. *Necâtî Bey Divanı.* Available via the Ottoman Text Archive Project, http://courses.washington.edu/otap/archive/data/arch_txt/texts/a_necati1.html.

Niyazioğlu, Aslı. 2016. *Dreams and Lives in Ottoman Istanbul: A Seventeenth Century Biographer's Perspective (Birmingham Byzantine and Ottoman Studies).* London: Routledge.

Peirce, Leslie. 1993. *The Imperial Harem: Women and Sovereignty in the Ottoman Empire.* New York: Oxford Univ. Press.

Revânî. *Revânî Divanı.* 1986. Edited by Ziya Avşar. Ankara: Kültür ve Turizm Bakanlığı Yayınları.

Roded, Ruth. 1994. *Women in Islamic Biographical Collections: From Ibn Sa'd to Who's Who*. Boulder, CO: Rienner.

Rosenthal, Margaret. 1992. *The Honest Cortesan: Veronica Franco, Citizen and Writer in the Sixteenth-Century Venice*. Chicago: Univ. of Chicago Press.

El-Rouayheb, Khaled. 2005. *Before Homosexuality in the Arab-Islamic World, 1500–1800*. Chicago: Univ. of Chicago Press.

Schick, Irvin C. 2010. "The Harem as Gendered Space and Spatial Reproduction of Gender." In *From Harem Histories*, edited by Marilyn Booth, 69–86. Durham, NC: Duke Univ. Press.

———. 2011. "Print Capitalism and Women's Sexual Agency in Late Ottoman Empire." *Comparative Studies of South Asia, Africa and the Middle East* 31 (1): 196–216.

Schimmel, Annemarie. 1975. *Mystical Dimensions of Islam*. Chapel Hill: Univ. of North Carolina Press.

———. 1997. *My Soul Is a Woman: The Feminine in Islam*. Translated by Susan Ray. New York: Continuum.

Segol, Marla. 2009. "Representing the Body in Poems by Medieval Muslim Women." *Medieval Feminist Forum: A Journal of Gender and Sexuality* 45 (1): 147–69.

Sehî Bey. 1978. *Heşt Behişt*. Edited by Günay Kut. Cambridge, MA: Harvard Univ. Press.

Sezer, Şennur. 2005. *Türk Safo'su Mihri Hatun*. Istanbul: Kapı Yayınları.

Sharma, Sunil. 2009. "From Aesha to Nur Jahan: The Shaping of a Classical Persian Poetic Canon of Women." *Journal of Persianate Studies* 2 (2): 147–64.

Silay, Kemal. 1997. "Singing His Words: Ottoman Women Poets and the Power of Patriarchy." In *Women in the Ottoman Empire: Middle Eastern Women in the Early Modern Era*, edited by Madeline C. Zilfi, 197–213. Leiden: Brill.

Sperl, Stefan, and Yorgos Dedes. 2013. "In the Rose-Bower Every Leaf is a Page of Delicate Meaning: An Arabic Perspective on Three Ottoman Kasides" [Her Varak Bir Nüktedir Gülşende: Üç Osmanlı Kasidesine Ar ap Kasidesi Açısından Bir Bakış].

In *Eski Türk Edebiyatı Çalışmaları/Kasideye Medhiyye: biçime, işleve ve muhtevaya ait tespitler*, edited by Hatice Aynur, Müjgan Çakır, Hanife Koncu, Selim Kuru, and Ali Emre Özyıldırım, 188–314. Istanbul: Klasik.

Stetkevych, Suzanne. 1993. *The Mute Immortals Speak: Pre-Islamic Poetry and Poetics of Ritual*. Ithaca, NY: Cornell Univ. Press.

———. 2013. "Performative Poetics in Abbasid Poetry." *Japan Association for Middle East Studies* 29 (2): 107–43.

Szuppe, Maria. 1996. "The Female Intellectual Milieu in Timurid and Post Timurid Herat: Faxri Heravi's Biography of Poetesses, Javaher al-Ajayeb." *Oriento Moderno* 15 (2): 119–37.

Terzioğlu, Derin. 1995. "The Imperial Circumcision Festival of 1582: An Interpretation." *Muqarnas: An Annual on Islamic Art and Architecture* 12: 84–100.

Tolasa, Harun. 1983. *Sehi, Latifi, Aşık Çelebi Tezkirelerine göre 16. Yüzyılda Edebiyat Araştırma ve Eleştirisi*. İzmir: Ege Univ.

Toska, Zehra. 2006. "Divan Şiirinde Kadın Şairlerin Sesi." In *Türk Edebiyatı Tarihi*, 663–74. Ankara: Kültür ve Turizm Bakanlığı Yayınları.

Woolf, Virginia. (1929) 2012. *A Room of One's Own*. Reprint, Los Angeles: IndoEuropean Publishing.

Ze'evi, Dror. 2006. *Producing Desire: Changing Sexual Discourse in the Ottoman Middle East, 1500–1900*. Berkeley: Univ. of California Press.

Zilfi, Madeline C., ed. 1997. *Women in the Ottoman Empire: Middle Eastern Women in the Early Modern Era*. Leiden: Brill.

Index

Page numbers appearing in italics refer to photographs and tables.

Didem Havlioğlu is lecturing fellow in the Department of Asian and Middle Eastern Studies at Duke University. Her research focuses on Ottoman intellectual history and gender and sexuality in Ottoman culture production. She is particularly interested in women poets and writers and their ways of appropriating traditional discourses. Havlioğlu holds a doctoral degree from the University of Washington.